Judith Butler

Judith Butler's work on gender, sexuality, identity, and the body has proved massively influential in contemporary feminist theory, and lesbian and gay studies, as well as across a range of academic disciplines in the humanities and social sciences. It is also notoriously difficult to access. This book provides a comprehensive and accessible introduction to Butler's work, plus a critical examination of it and its precursors, both feminist (including Simone de Beauvoir, Monique Wittig, Julia Kristeva and Luce Irigaray), and non-feminist (including Erving Goffman, Michel Foucault, Jacques Lacan, and Jacques Derrida). Butler's account of gender as performance and performative is examined as it has developed in her work and the shifting relation to psycho-analysis is discussed. The implications of her ideas for understanding subjectivity, agency and political practice are explored, along with the possibilities for social change and transformation. Other topics covered include:

- sociological notions of performance
- the materiality of the body and the role of biology
- power, identity and social regulation
- melancholia and gender identity
- hate speech, pornography and 'race'
- transgender and sexual difference

This well-written text will be of great interest to undergraduate and graduate students alike in the many disciplines in which Butler's work has become influential, including gender and women's studies, philosophy, cultural studies, literary criticism, law and sociology. It will also prove valuable to research students and scholars working in the fields of gender, sexuality, the body, and identity.

Gill Jagger is a lecturer in the department of Social Sciences at the University of Hull. Her research interests include poststructuralist theory and gender, sexual difference and the body and she has published in these areas. She co-edited *Changing Family Values* (Routledge, 1999).

Judith Butler

Sexual politics, social change and the
power of the performative

Gill Jagger

Routledge
Taylor & Francis Group

LONDON AND NEW YORK

First published 2008
by Routledge
2 Park Square, Milton Park, Abingdon, Oxon OX14 4RN

Simultaneously published in the USA and Canada
by Routledge
270 Madison Ave, New York, NY 10016

*Routledge is an imprint of the Taylor & Francis Group,
an Informa business*

© 2008 Gill Jagger

Typeset in Sabon by
RefineCatch Limited, Bungay, Suffolk

British Library Cataloguing in Publication Data
A catalogue record for this book is available from the British Library

Library of Congress Cataloging in Publication Data
Jagger, Gill, 1965–
    Judith Butler: sexual politics, social change and the power of the
performative / Gill Jagger.
       p. cm.
    Includes bibliographical references and index.
    1. Feminist theory. 2. Butler, Judith, 1956–Criticism and
interpretation. 3. Sex role–Philosophy. I. Title
    HQ1190.J346 2008
    301.092—dc22   2007032458

ISBN 10: 0–415–21974–4 (hbk)
ISBN 10: 0–415–21975–2 (pbk)
ISBN 10: 0–203–93190–4 (ebk)

ISBN13: 978–0–415–21974–7 (hbk)
ISBN13: 978–0–415–21975–4 (pbk)
ISBN13: 978–0–203–93190–5 (ebk)

Contents

Introduction   1

1 Gender as performance and performative   17

2 Body matters: from construction to materialization   51

3 Performativity, subjection and the possibility of agency   89

4 The politics of the performative: hate speech,
  pornography and 'race'   115

5 Beyond identity politics: gender, transgender and
  sexual difference   137

  Afterword   159

  Notes   163
  Bibliography   171
  Index   181

Introduction

In her account of performativity, Judith Butler provides an influential analysis of sex, gender, sexuality and the body. It represents a major contribution to feminist gender theory and is often regarded as providing a founding contribution to 'queer theory', which was newly emerging in the 1990s when *Gender Trouble* was first published. Butler's work combines aspects of feminist theory and philosophy, lesbian and gay studies, and queer theory, as well as increasingly drawing on aspects of psychoanalysis. At the same time, it builds on a broadly poststructuralist understanding of subjectivity, rooted in the work of Michel Foucault and, to some extent, Jacques Derrida, Friedrich Nietzsche and Jacques Lacan.[1] It involves a radical critique of identity categories in which not only gender, but also sex, sexuality and the body are conceived as cultural products. Butler thus draws on the work of an eclectic range of theorists and theoretical traditions in *Gender Trouble* and *Bodies that Matter* to challenge the naturalization of sex, gender, the body and (hetero)sexuality; and to highlight the role of what she terms 'compulsory heterosexuality' and, following Irigaray, 'phallogocentrism' in the production of these categories.

She is concerned, in particular, to reveal the ways in which sex and gender are produced within a binary framework that is *conditioned* by heterosexuality, rather than the other way around. In other words, it is argued that it is not that sex and gender produce heterosexuality but that heterosexuality produces sex and gender in a binary form. Basically, then, Butler is rejecting an account of gender in which femininity and masculinity are taken to be the cultural articulation of a biological sex.

She argues instead that there is nothing given about gender, nor is there any pre-cultural or pre-discursive sex that provides the basis for its cultural construction. In fact, she argues that the category of sex is itself a gendered category. The sex/gender distinction, which allowed early second-wave feminists to avoid and challenge biological determinism and to examine the cultural production of gender, is thus rejected as inadequate to understanding the performativity of gender.

Indeed, *Gender Trouble* was initially an attempt to intervene in feminist gender theory, as Butler remarks in an interview in *Radical Philosophy* (Butler 1994b), and involves an attempt to move beyond the sex/gender distinction that had become central to (Anglo-American and Australian) feminist theory during the 1970s and early 1980s. This distinction underpinned the 'essentialism versus constructionism' debates that are often taken to characterize that period, and had been useful in early attempts to denaturalize gender and avoid biological determinism – the view that 'biology is destiny' – by highlighting the cultural diversity in constructions of masculinity and femininity. However, the sex/gender distinction does still seem to involve posing gender as some sort of cultural overlay on a basic biological category that is taken as given. As such, it came to be seen as problematic for many later feminists, such as Butler, who were more concerned with deconstructing this kind of binary opposition. Indeed, in *Gender Trouble*, Butler is rather concerned to examine the ways in which the categories of sex and/or gender come to be *established* as foundational and to analyse their pivotal role in the institution of 'compulsory heterosexuality'. Although in the 1990s there was a resurgence of arguments for radically separating gender from sexuality amongst queer theorists, Butler argued against this move.[2] Her aim, as she points out in 'Critically Queer' in *Bodies that Matter*, is rather to rethink this distinction in terms of 'a set of non-causal relations' that can somehow accommodate the inter-implication of gender and sexuality (and feminism and queer theory) without reducing either aspect to the other; to establish 'their constitutive inter-relationship' (Butler 1993a: 240). Moreover, this needs to be done in a way that can allow for the need to interrogate 'the formation of each in specified racial regimes and geopolitical spatializations' (p. 240). Her notion of the performativity of gender is an attempt to do this.

Her basic premise, as she puts it in any early paper, is that embodied selves 'do not pre-exist the cultural conventions which essentially signify bodies' (Butler 1988: 526) but rather 'the foundational categories of identity – the binary of sex, gender and the body – can be shown as productions that *create the effect* of the natural, the original and the inevitable' (Butler 1990a: viii, my emphasis). Hence she wants to expose these foundational categories and desire as 'effects of a specific formation of power' (1990a: x), in a Foucauldian/Nietzschean sense. She wants to reveal the ways in which 'the regulatory norms of sex' work in a performative fashion in the service of the 'heterosexual matrix', as it is described in *Gender Trouble*, but which becomes 'heterosexual hegemony' in *Bodies that Matter*.

One of the starting points of this account is Simone de Beauvoir's claim that 'one is not born a woman but becomes one', which is set in the context of Foucault's view of the body and subjectivity as effects of power and normalization. Butler builds on the Foucauldian notion that subjectivity is discursively produced and that this does not involve the notion of a pre-existing subject *on* whom power and discourses act, but rather that subjects are formed *through* their discursively constituted identity. She develops the notion of performativity to explain how this works in relation to gendered subjectivity, an aspect which Foucault himself did not really consider, and also to allow for the possibility of resistance and change without succumbing to the limitations of his work in this area (as discussed in Chapter 1 and again in Chapter 3).

Butler also draws on lesbian and gay perspectives in her otherwise very Foucauldian account of sexuality as a discursive product. These are employed to suggest that heterosexuality is a matter of imitation and parody, rather than a natural product of sexed and gendered bodies and, as such, it is essentially unstable. Indeed, it is this instability that enables the possibility of resistance and change in her account. Butler also draws on the insights of gay and lesbian sexuality, and desire, to suggest that reproductive heterosexuality is a normative ideal and, as such, fictional. She argues that it is revealed as a fiction by gender discontinuities in lesbian, gay, bisexual and heterosexual contexts in which gender does not necessarily follow from sex, and desire and sexuality do not seem to follow from gender (as discussed in Chapter 1). This normative ideal creates a false sense of stability and coherence that works in the interests of reproductive heterosexuality and serves to conceal the discontinuities which undermine the expressive model of gender identity on which it is based.

Butler's approach, therefore, involves analysing the performative production of sexed identity, concentrating in *Gender Trouble* on the processes through which sex and gender come to be conceived as natural extensions of a biological body, rather than taking the materiality (or biology) of the body as a starting point. In *Bodies that Matter*, in an attempt to answer accusations that she neglects the materiality of the body in *Gender Trouble*, she develops her account of performativity in the context of Derrida's reworking of speech act theory to focus on the ways in which bodies are *materialized* as sexed. This is a crucial move, as the adaptation of speech act theory is an important feature of her account of performativity and it makes her approach significantly different from theatrical models of performance (as discussed in Chapter 1). It allows her to link the materialization of the body to the performativity of gender and, in so doing, rethink the materiality of the sex/gendered body in non-essential terms. Indeed, she argues that this view of the body, as a matter of materialization, involves rethinking the meaning of social construction beyond that implied in the essentialism versus constructionism dichotomy (as discussed in Chapter 2).

Butler also draws on psychoanalysis even though she is highly critical of some aspects of it. As she says in one interview, she does not 'think one can offer an account of how sexuality is formed without psychoanalysis' but she also thinks that psychoanalysis contributes to 'the forming of sexuality' in the binary framework of 'compulsory heterosexuality' (Butler 1994a: 36). In *Gender Trouble* aspects of both Freud's and Lacan's work are thus employed to help in the denaturalization of identity categories. However, their theories are also subjected to a Foucauldian critique to highlight the heterosexist assumptions on which they too are based. Moreover, in *Bodies that Matter* Foucault's critique of the repressive hypothesis – that is, the idea that sexuality is somehow innate but repressed – is linked to a critique of a Lacanian account of subjectivity. Butler takes from this the idea that identity involves multiple and co-existing identifications and that gender identifications are 'phantasmatic'. As such, she argues, they are not something which is given in biology, or some sort of essential self. They are rather impossible to embody.

Indeed, Butler becomes increasingly concerned with the psychic aspects of identity and the role of social regulation and power in the formation of this. In *The Psychic Life of Power* (Butler 1997b) she returns to Hegel, who was a key focus in her first book, *Subjects of Desire* (Butler 1987a). In *The Psychic Life of Power* she develops a theory of subjection based on an adaptation of Hegel on the 'unhappy consciousness', in the *Phenomenology of Spirit*, in conjunction with a development of Althusser's theory of interpellation, and a reading of Freud and Foucault. The concern here is with how social regulation works through the 'psychic incorporation' of norms. This becomes a question of the workings of desire: how the subjection of desire becomes the desire for subjection. It involves examining the ways that subjection involves both subordination to power and the production of 'passionate attachments' to identity categories (as discussed in Chapter 3).

This book charts the development of Butler's ideas and the implications they have for feminist theory and political practice and, to a lesser extent, queer theory. It is intended as a critical introduction to Butler's work, and the responses it has generated. Hence, her ideas are situated in the context of contemporary feminist concerns, and some of the significance of the differences between her approach and other 'queer' perspectives is highlighted. However, it must be emphasized that this book neither aims nor claims to speak for Butler. Although I have tried to produce a fair account of the development of Butler's theory of performativity, as well as a critical analysis of it, it must be acknowledged that this is, and can only be, a partial account; as such, it is necessarily selective. It is also my particular interpretation. Furthermore, if at times I have presented Butler's ideas in ways that would seem to go against the grain of one of the key theoretical insights of her approach, which emphasizes the problems of determining 'proper objects', this has been done in the interests of exposition. It is not intended to undermine those insights in any way, nor to assert 'proper objects' in relation to Butler's work, but rather to provide a starting point from which to begin to engage with it.

Moreover, there are so many influences on Butler's work that it is impossible to do justice to them all, so I have concentrated on those that are the most significant, in one way or another, in terms of the themes and issues of this book. These are: the relationship between language, reference and materiality; sex, gender, sexuality and the body; power, identity and social regulation; subjectivity, agency and feminist political practice; the politics of the performative; and social change and transformation.

It is argued that one of the main strengths of Butler's attempt to theorize gendered embodiment lies in the refusal to accept the notion of sexual difference as irreducible and to conceive it rather as something that is socially instituted to function as irreducible. This is important because much feminist theory is concerned with rethinking the body to acknowledge the significance of sexual difference in the production of embodied subjectivity, whilst also avoiding essentialist understandings of sexed bodies; and there is some agreement that this involves focusing on representation and the symbolic as intrinsic aspects of the production of social and material reality. One point of divergence, however, between Butler's account and others stems from the extent to which this involves some kind of reconstructive project around the bodies of women. This is Irigaray's move and that of her followers, as well as many others (e.g. Braidotti 1994; Grosz 1994; Kristeva 1982; Clement and Kristeva 2003). Such a move, however, stands in danger of reifying the binarized notion of sexual difference on which heterosexuality (and the Lacanian symbolic) is based. Butler rejects such a move in her notion of gender as performance and performative.

Butler's focus is rather on the heterosexualizing force of the symbolic order and language. She examines the political effects of grounding the category of woman in the materiality of bodies and posing the materiality of sex as causal. She argues that one of the effects of this is the production of the duality of bodies that sustains reproductive heterosexuality as a compulsory order. Moreover, she argues in *Bodies that Matter* and *Feminist Contentions* that sexual difference is no more primary than other aspects of social difference, 'nor is its formation under-standable outside of a complex mapping of social power' (1995a: 142). In which case, striving to establish an autonomous female sexuality is not necessarily helpful (as discussed in Chapter 2).

Furthermore, Butler's notion of the performativity of identity categories also avoids some of the limitations in the work of certain (male) theorists of 'reflexive identity transformation' that became popular in contemporary social theory in the 1990s (e.g. Giddens 1992; Featherstone 1992). These accounts are also concerned with the role of representation and the symbolic in the constitution of identity. However, as McNay argues, they tend to place too much emphasis on 'the expressive possibilities thrown up by processes of detraditionalization' (McNay 1999: 95) because they do not adequately address the embodied pre-reflexive aspects of identity formation. It is precisely these aspects that Butler is trying to accommodate in *The Psychic Life of Power*, and to some extent in *Excitable Speech*. In these works she examines the ways in which the pre-reflexive, embodied aspects of identity are linguistically instituted, and intrinsic to the process of *assujetissement* (becoming both a subject and subjected), in order to render them resilient, but not necessarily immutable; and to argue that they are historical and cultural products rather than biological or psychological givens (as dis-cussed in Chapter 3).

An important aspect of Butler's critique of identity is that the categories through which embodied subjects come into being are never fully determining. This allows for the possibility of resistance, for the rearticulation of the categories, and hence social and self-transformation. Moreover, as these categories are themselves linguistically constituted, rather than naturally given, the way of approaching change and transformation is through language and signification – through the significatory practices that constitute and constrain particular identities, bodies and selves.

However, it is this aspect of Butler's work that has probably caused the most controversy and attracted the most criticism. The view of resistance and change entailed in her account of performativity has proved problematic for feminist projects because it is based on an account of subjectivity that has signifi-cant implications for traditional understandings of the concepts of agency and critique (as discussed in Chapter 1). Since subjectivity is rethought as a product of language and signification, the root to change is also considered to be through language and signification, and agency is rethought in linguistic terms. It becomes 'discursive' or 'linguistic' agency. All this has proved problematic for feminist projects, and indeed others, where the aim is to develop concrete political programmes. Although Butler insists on the political significance of her work, the political elements are thus problematic, not least in that they do not conform to traditional ideas about the scope and practice of the political but rather highlight the problems with traditional understandings of this. These are key issues in Butler's work and they are a guiding thread in each of the chapters of this book.

The book is organized into five chapters. Chapter 1 begins by examining Butler's account of gender as a performance, which is performative as expressed in *Gender Trouble*, and the denaturalization and critique of identity categories that this involves. It examines the claim that there is no pre-discursive sex and that, contrary to the naturalist fallacy in which gender is somehow *caused* by sex, it is rather discourses of gender that produce sex as a causal category. Without these discourses, and the acts to which they give rise, there would be no gender and the gendered body has no ontological status outside of those acts. These are clearly radical views, and in many ways counter-intuitive, so it's not surprising that much controversy followed from the publication of *Gender Trouble*. Some of these controversies are also examined in this chapter. Initial areas of contention stemmed from the suggestion that gender is a performance in a theatrical sense and, as such, is subject to change at will; and the assumption that as a social construct gender becomes a mere arbitrary artifice that can easily be dispensed with. These interpretations are interrogated in Chapter 1 through an examination of the distinction between performance in a theatrical sense and performance in a performative sense, drawing on an early paper entitled 'Performative Acts and Gender Constitution' (Butler 1988). Butler's account of performativity is compared with the dramaturgical models of subjectivity employed in earlier phenomenological and sociological work, and distinguished from them. This distinction is crucial to Butler's account of performativity and once it is appreciated, voluntarist interpretations are no longer sustainable.

However this isn't the end of the matter; rather it is the start of another set of controversies. Once it is appreciated that this account of the performativity of identity categories, such as sex and gender, is based on a combination of speech act theory and a poststructuralist understanding of subjectivity, in a Nietzschean sense in which there is no 'doer behind the deed', the possibility of agency would seem to be called into question and with it the potential for resistance and change. At the same time, the bodily basis of identity and the category 'woman' are also rendered problematic, which would seem to undermine the possibility of identity politics, on which much feminist and queer theory and activism is based, and to challenge the rationale for any specifically feminist theory or practice based on the experiences or bodies of women. This also adds to the confusion about the political possibilities of performativity. On top of this, *Gender Trouble* seems to suggest a politics of parody for which drag is the model and to equate the denaturalization of sex and gender with a kind of instability that is inherently subversive. All of these controversies are examined in this chapter.

It is argued that Butler's critique of gender categories does not gesture towards a post-gender position, as is sometimes claimed, as if it were possible to simply step outside of gender categories. It rather involves demonstrating the simultaneous necessity and contingency of identity categories, and highlighting the ways in which agency needs to be reformulated to retain the possibility of resistance and change. Although much has to be done to develop Butler's account of performativity to more clearly allow for these possibilities in her later work, the possibility of agency, and the potential for resistance and change, are key themes throughout in Butler's work and, as such, remain prominent themes in all of the chapters of this book. Furthermore, although her later work develops many of the ideas in *Gender Trouble* in highly significant ways, this early account of identity categories contains a number of basic ideas that do not significantly change. These are identified in this chapter.

The main focus of Chapter 2 is the 'matter' of the body. This is often perceived as a particularly problematic area of Butler's account of performativity. The main problems stem from the fact that it leaves no role for the body in its material or corporeal specificity, either in the social and political construction of identity categories, or as a source of resistance and change, because it too becomes a performative effect; a socially constructed product of the effects of power and social regulation. Indeed, Butler explicitly takes up the issue of the materiality of the body in *Bodies that Matter* in response to criticisms that it is neglected in *Gender Trouble*. In the former, she highlights the problems with taking the materiality of bodies as the starting point of a process of social construction, as something that pre-exists particular constructions. She suggests that rather than taking the materiality of the body as the starting point of feminist theories, which would involve colluding in the process of construction and reifying politically constructed categories, what is required is a critical genealogy of the concept of materiality. The main features of this move are examined in this chapter.

Particular attention is given to Butler's attempt to avoid posing the matter of bodies and the process of construction as oppositional, as in a materiality/construction dichotomy, and the view of the body as a product of a process of materialization through which bodies are constituted as sexed, as well as classed and raced. This reconceptualization of materiality allows her to focus on ways in which the category of sex is not immutable but is rather produced as a normative constraint. Hence the category of sex becomes a cultural norm through which bodies are materialized in *Bodies that Matter*. Feminist criticisms of this account of materiality and Butler's responses to these are also examined.

This understanding of materiality also involves the development of Butler's account of performativity through Derrida's reworking of speech act theory and the notions of iterability and citationality involved in that, as well as a further engagement with aspects of psychoanalysis, especially the notions of identification and morphogenesis. Both of these developments are examined in this Chapter 2. Butler's most salient criticism of psychoanalytic accounts of sexual difference, gender and desire is that they are premised on an implicit framework of normative heterosexuality. She seeks to challenge and avoid this in her adaptation of psychoanalytic insights. This criticism is explained and examined with a particular focus on Butler's account of gender identifications as 'phantasmatic', and the way in which she draws on Lacan's account of sex and sexed identity as symbolic positions. This use of Lacan involves rejecting his account of the fixity of the phallus as the founding moment in the symbolic order. This is done by setting it in the context of Derrida's critique of speech act theory, and the notion of iterability. This allows her to argue that, notwithstanding the contemporary privileging of the phallus, it is, nevertheless, always in a process of signification and resignification. As such, the phallus is not so much the founding moment of the symbolic order, as Lacan would have it, but rather a part of a reiterable signifying practice. This then provides the possibility for change, for the resignification of the imaginary and thus of alternative sexed identifications and body morphologies. The significance of these ideas for developing strategies for change is also considered in this chapter, and Butler's strategies are compared with those of Irigaray and Kristeva.

In relation to the materiality of the body, particular attention is paid to Butler's claim that this account of the materialization of bodies does not involve the suggestion that bodies are immaterial. It is rather to emphasize the materiality of significations and the regulatory frameworks through which embodied subjects achieve cultural intelligibility (or not). It is argued that Butler's account of performativity and the materialization of the body involves an application of the kind of critique that Derrida and Nietzsche make of Western metaphysics, to the feminist and queer problematic of sex, gender and the body. Hence, rather than denying the reality of materiality as critics tend to claim, the focus is on the role of language and signification (and the exclusions, repudiations and unthought) in the production of any apparent reality *in its materiality*: in this case the materiality of the body in what is taken to be its simply given and obvious corporeal specificity.

However, Butler's feminist and queer concerns differ from those of Derrida and Nietzsche in that she aims to reveal that the significations and regulatory frameworks through which embodied subjects come into being are shaped by a symbolic order that is both phallocentric and heterosexist. Furthermore, it depends for its stability on the exclusion and repudiation of the abject of heterosexuality. Hence the importance of the psychoanalytic categories of identification and morphology, suitably adapted, which allow her to focus on the role of the heterosexist imperative in the materialization of bodies, enabling certain sexed identifications and excluding others.

Chapter 3 returns to the issue of agency in Butler's account of performativity, in the context of her account of the 'psychic incorporation of norms' in *The Psychic Life of Power*. The broad aim of this move, in which Butler continues to draw on psychoanalytic concepts, is to theorize the relationship between the psychic aspects of identity and social power and regulation in order to account for the intractability of identity categories, whilst at the same time continuing to allow for the possibility of resistance and change. It also involves rethinking the relationship between interiority and exteriority in her account of performativity. Foucault's view of power as productive of subjectivity is thus rethought through the psychoanalytic concepts of foreclosure and melancholic incorporation; as well as through a further development of Althusser's concept of interpellation and a revision of Hegel's concept of recognition. These theorists, and Nietzsche, all develop accounts of subjectivity as necessarily involving a form of subjection – subjection, that is, to social power and regulation. Butler adapts these insights in the context of her feminist and queer concerns with sexed identity to theorize the way that social norms and regulation are in operation in the formation of the psyche. This is important for her account of resistance and change. It provides a way of theorizing the intractability of identity categories without making them entirely determining. This is because the psychic incorporation of norms involves the production of 'passionate attachments' (in a Freudian sense), which cannot be simply disregarded, as it is through these that we come into existence (in a Hegelian sense, involving recognition). But it also involves the view, against Freud and Lacan, that this psychic regulation is historical and social and, as such, contingent and changeable. The point now is that identity is only achieved through constitutive exclusions and that while these operate through the psyche they are also political, involving regulation and authority. Politics therefore needs to address the issue of identification even though, in this view, we cannot simply discard the identities we have become.

These moves are examined in Chapter 3, focusing in particular on the implications they have for feminist political practice. This involves examining the significance they have for Butler's account of agency. Indeed, one of Butler's expressed intentions in *The Psychic Life of Power* is to further develop her account of agency. It also involves examining criticisms that the view of resistance in Butler's account of performativity is more of an abstract potentiality than a concrete possibility, and the issue of the relationship between Butler's work and concrete political practice. This has been a sticking point for some commentators from the beginning. The problem is that whilst Butler's theoretical account of the intractability of identity categories in *The Psychic Life of Power* does allow for the possibility of resistance and change, this development does nothing to help the thorny problem of how to operationalize that resistance, whether in individual terms or in the context of feminist political programmes. If anything, this issue is even more problematic in this theoretical framework, given the significance of the unconscious and the role of foreclosure and exclusions in the constitution of identity. Although these developments provide significant insights into the political nature of identity, these same insights thus pose further problems for developing a politics of identity and commonality. These issues are interrogated and explained by setting them in the context of Butler's debate with Žižek in *Contingency, Universality, Hegemony* (Butler *et al.* 2000).

Chapter 4 continues to focus on the political potential of Butler's account of performativity, and the possibilities for resistance and change that it involves in what are more clearly concrete situations. These are the debates in the US around the regulation of 'hate speech' that Butler discusses in *Excitable Speech* (Butler 1997a). She argues against the use of speech act theory in these debates, focusing in particular on declarations of homosexuality in the military, racist hate speech and pornography. This involves further engagement with Althusser's account of interpellation (continuing some of the themes of *The Psychic Life of Power*) in order to elaborate on the 'linguistic vulnerability' at the heart of subjectivity, as well as the (paradoxical) possibilities for resistance and change that this represents. It also involves further discussion of her account of 'linguistic' or 'discursive' agency. These developments are discussed in this chapter.

The main focus is on the difference between Butler's account of speech act theory and the way that this is employed in the hate speech debates in the US. This stems from Butler's insistence that although we are in some sense linguistically *constituted*, it does not necessarily follow from this that we are linguistically *determined*, either by the performative force of racist hate speech or pornographic representations conceived as hate speech, or, indeed, any other forms of hate speech. This is an important distinction to grasp when evaluating Butler's work as, despite the focus on language and speech acts, she attempts to avoid both nominalism and determinism, as the discussions in previous chapters make clear. This distinction is underlined in *Excitable Speech* because of the 'excitability' and temporality of speech acts. This renders them out of control and unpredictable, as well as open-ended and citational, and thus continually in need of iteration and reiteration. Therefore, it might be through speech acts that we come into being, because they confer social existence, but those speech acts must be repeated and, since that repetition is not merely mechanical, this always involves the possibility of appropriation and reiteration in unintended ways.

Hence, despite Butler's own emphasis on the performativity of 'speech', she nevertheless resists the move to conflate speech with conduct, which the hate speech legislation requires. This would be to succumb to the 'the fantasy of sovereign power in speech' which, she argues, underpins the work of Austin and Althusser. Butler argues that the injurious aspects of hate speech cannot be fixed in the speech act itself, or the intentions or authority of the speaker, as this fantasy suggests, precisely because speech acts are 'excitable' – i.e. their meanings and/or effects are out of the control of the speaker so they cannot be fixed by their intentions. This means that there is always the possibility for the speech act to perform alternative meanings to those that are expressly intended. Butler emphasizes the possibilities for resistance that stem from this 'excitability' in relation to hate speech in *Excitable Speech*. This stems from the potential for the resignification of the conventional meanings that the excitability of speech acts, including those that are hateful, presents. It is Butler's focus on this potential that is at the root of her disagreement with the various protagonists in the hate speech debates who, she argues, accord too much determinism and too much power to the words to 'wound', and not enough recognition of the enabling aspects of speech acts, however injurious.

These themes and issues are examined in Chapter 4, focusing in particular on Butler's analysis of racist hate speech and her account of 'racialization', and her analysis of pornography as hate speech in the work of Catharine MacKinnon. It is argued that these moves mark a significant development in her theory of performativity by demonstrating the unintended, and often reactionary, performative force of political utterance, as well as the limitations of censorship as exemplified in relation to racist language, pornographic representations of women, and homophobia. Butler's analyses show how all of these work due to the existence of conventional power relations rather than the particular speech acts of racist, misogynistic and/or homophobic individuals or groups. Developing the theory of performativity in this context thus also makes a significant contribution to critical race theory, and to debates within feminism about pornography.

Chapter 5 returns to the issue of the materiality of the body and many of the concerns that were discussed in Chapter 2. In particular, the political implications of Butler's view of the body as a performative effect of regimes of power/discourse; the shift that her account of performativity requires away from identity politics, based on sameness and commonality, to a politics of identity, which takes more account of the exclusions on which any particular identity is based; the significance of the duality of sexual difference for understanding sex, gender and the body; and criticisms that Butler's account of performativity neglects the materiality or corporeality of the body. These issues are interrogated in this chapter in relation to transgender and transsexuality (trans), as trans experiences also clearly present a challenge to the duality of sexual difference and the binary system of sex and gender that it sustains.

The significance of Butler's account of performativity and politics of identity for trans theories and politics is thus examined. At the same time, the significance of transgender and transsexuality for Butler's account of performativity, and the view of resistance and change that it involves, is also considered. Particular attention is paid to the criticism that Butler's account of the body neglects the significance of the materiality of the trans body as a causal factor in trans experience and identity, focusing on the work of Jay Prosser (1998); and to the significance of trans identity for Butler's critique of sexual difference in any sort of essential binary form. In relation to the latter, whilst it may indeed be clear that making sense of trans experiences presents a challenge to the duality of sexual difference and the binary system of sex and gender that it maintains, it is not at all clear to what extent this involves either transgressing this system (if at all) or capitulating to it. This issue is examined by setting the tension between the goals of transgressive trans politics and those of trans people whose aim is to pass as the other sex, in the context of Butler's account of the materiality of the body as a performative effect. The implications of trans experience for theorizing the relationship between sex, gender and the body in terms of body image is also considered in the context of Butler's account of performativity. It is argued that when trans experiences are considered in this way, they seem to undermine accounts of the body that are based on imaginary schemata that are rooted in the duality of sexual difference, as in the work of Moira Gatens and Elizabeth Grosz. It is rather that trans experiences and politics could contribute in some way to what Butler describes as the 'remapping of sexual difference' and help towards the rearticulation of the hegemonic symbolic beyond the binary frame.

Furthermore, Butler's account of performativity is criticized as politically debilitating if there is no independently existing body on which to base our feminist and queer projects and there are no independent truths of sex, gender and sexuality on which we can build our identity, including trans identity; not even the duality of sexual difference. However, the point is that just as such universal truths have been undermined in contemporary social theory, so Butler's genealogical critique shows this to be equally the case in relation to the body, sex and gender. Political programmes need to address this 'fact' and Butler's account of performativity provides a way of theorizing the significance of this for rethinking sex, gender and sexuality; and a starting point for rethinking the binary frameworks that structure these, even if it doesn't seem possible to move beyond them.

1   Gender as performance and performative

Butler's account of gender as a kind of performance that is performative in *Gender Trouble* has proved highly influential in its critique of identity categories as a matter of social and political construction, rather than the expression of some kind of essential nature. However, it has also proved highly controversial as this critique extends beyond the category of gender to sex, sexuality and the body. Indeed, the stated aim of *Gender Trouble* is to establish a critical genealogy of the construction of the categories of sex, gender, sexuality, desire and the body as identity categories and reveal them, and the binary framework that structures them, to be products of 'compulsory' heterosexuality and 'phallogocentrism'. Butler wants to show that identity categories are 'fictional' products of these 'regimes of power/ knowledge' or 'power/discourse' (Butler 1990a: xi) rather than natural effects of the body. They are fictional in the sense that they do not pre-exist the regimes of power/knowledge but are performative products of them. They are performative in the sense that the categories themselves produce the identity they are deemed to be simply representing. Hence:

> A genealogical critique refuses to search for the origins of gender, the inner truth of female desire, a genuine or authentic sexual identity that repression has kept from view; rather genealogy investigates the political stakes in designating as an origin and cause those identity categories that are in fact the effects of institutions, practices, discourses with multiple and diffuse points of origin.
>
> (Butler 1990a: x–xi)

Thus Butler wants to show that these apparently foundational categories are actually cultural products that 'create the effect of the natural, the original, the inevitable' (p. viii). However, denaturalizing these categories is only one aspect of this genealogical critique. Another important aim is to destabilize the epistemological and ontological regimes that produce them as natural (p. xi). Hence, she goes on: 'The task of this inquiry is to centre on and decentre such defining institutions: phallogocentrism and compulsory heterosexuality' (p. xi). Significantly then, she is not just concerned with the denaturalization of identity categories but also with the possibilities for resistance and change within all this. She wants to reveal that heterosexuality, and the binary system of sexual difference on which it is based, is compulsory yet at the same time show that it is permanently unstable, and to argue that it is this instability that opens up the space for change.

Much of the controversy that arose from this critique of identity categories, however, stems from the same source: the model of subjectivity on which it is based and the implications of this for agency and critique, and resistance and change. This is because Butler's account of the performativity of gender is based on a poststructuralist understanding of the subject, rooted in a critique of the 'metaphysics of substance' in a Nietzschean sense, and the 'metaphysics of presence' in a Derridean sense. In this understanding, the substantive 'I' of the humanist subject becomes an illusion, a product of the grammatical structure of language rather than a unified, coherent being which linguistic categories simply represent. In Butler's application of this critique of the humanist subject to the problematic of identity in a feminist, and what was to become known as a 'queer', sense, identity categories become performative effects of language and signification, rather than properties of individuals, or the linguistic expression of 'nature', based on the materiality of the body. The political project thus becomes a matter of the subversion of identity rather than capitulation to those constructed categories by building theories and political programmes around them. Agency and critique, and resistance and change, become a matter of the subversion of identity. The subversion of identity becomes a matter of opening up the space for alternative significations and the displacement of the discursive regimes of compulsory heterosexuality and phallogocentrism. All this clearly has enormous implications for feminist and queer practice, not least because it involves a critique of the kind of identity politics on which much feminist and queer activism is based. It also appears to challenge the rationale for any specifically feminist theory based on the experiences or bodies of women, and any specifically queer theory based on the materiality of gay, lesbian or trans bodies.

Another related source of controversy stems from the notion of performance involved in Butler's account of performativity. There are two particular aspects to this. One is that it was often taken to involve the idea that gender is a performance in a theatrical sense and so could be changed at will. This was a view that tended to be embraced positively by some queer theorists but rejected in the main by feminists. The other stemmed from the assumption by some that as a socially constructed performance, gender becomes a mere arbitrary artifice. However, neither of these was a view to which Butler herself subscribed. Indeed, she actively argues against such interpretations as the discussion that follows will show. Nevertheless, as they were fairly common interpretations, they warrant some consideration when examining the early account of performativity that can be gleaned from *Gender Trouble*.

There was also some controversy around the critique of heterosexuality as a 'regulatory fiction' which seemed to suggest a politics of parody, for which drag was the model, and to equate instability with subversion. Although suggesting that instability provides the opportunity for resistance and change (for resignification) is not the same as saying that instability is itself subversive, nevertheless, this is something that Butler is often taken to be claiming and her account of subversion in *Gender Trouble* has attracted much criticism.

Despite all these controversies however, and others yet to be mentioned, Butler's critique of identity categories in *Gender Trouble* contains a number of elements that have not changed as she has developed her account of performativity in subsequent works. The theory of performativity involved becomes much more explicitly based on speech act theory (as discussed in Chapters 3 and 5) and psychoanalysis plays a greater role in explaining the intractability of identity categories (as discussed in Chapter 3). Nevertheless, the basic premise on which the critique of identity categories in *Gender Trouble* is based remains the same: there is nothing given about gender nor is there any pre-cultural or pre-discursive sex that provides the basis for its cultural construction. Identity is rather an effect of signifying practices rooted in regimes of power/knowledge characterized as compulsory heterosexuality and phallogocentrism. As such, it is a matter of social and political regulation rather than any sort of innate property of individuals, or source of agency in a traditional, liberal humanist sense. The political possibilities and agency stem from the inherent repeatability of these signifying practices and the possibility of resignification. Although the precise ways in which this works are given much more attention in her later work (Butler 1993a, 1997a, 1997b), the political aspirations continue to hinge on the possibilities of signification and resignification.

The main elements of Butler's account of performativity as expressed in *Gender Trouble* will thus be explained and the controversies they generate will be examined in this chapter. It will focus in particular on the following key themes: the distinction between gender as performance in a theatrical sense and gender as performance in a performative sense; the critique of heterosexuality as a matter of performance, imitation and drag; the issue of subversion and the role of parody as a political strategy; the constituted subject and the possibility of agency; and the critique of binary oppositions. The issue of the materiality of the body which has also generated much controversy is examined in detail in later chapters (in Chapter 2 in relation to feminism and in Chapter 5 in relation to queer theory and trans critiques), so it is only mentioned briefly here. Particular emphasis will be given, however, to the concept of resistance and change which, as I have argued, is a key issue for Butler throughout her work. It is also an aspect that attracts much criticism from critics and adherents alike.

Performance and performativity

In *Gender Trouble,* Butler argues that gender is a kind of enforced cultural performance, compelled by compulsory heterosexuality, and that, as such, it is performative. Rather than

expressing some inner core or pre-given identity, the performance of gender produces the *illusion* of such a core or essence.
This then becomes a cultural effect, a product of particular signifying practices, as we shall see. She also argues that there is
a temporal aspect to this performance as it involves the 'ritualized repetition of conventions', which are also 'shaped and
compelled by compulsory heterosexuality'. She refers to these
repetitions as 'sustained social performances' which create the
reality of gender, but which, significantly, are not separable from
agents, or actors, preceding the performances, as in a theatrical
model. Indeed, this inseparability is crucial to Butler's account
of performativity.

Nevertheless, one of the main causes of controversy in the
reception of *Gender Trouble* arose from the tendency to associ-
ate the notion of performance presented there with theatrical
models of subjectivity, which imply that there is an actor who
chooses which script to follow and then does the acting – and in
this sense is separable from the act. This, then, would seem to
imply voluntarism and the idea that there is some sort of everyday optionality about sex, gender and even the body.[1] Moreover, Butler's account of the performativity of gender does
involve a notion of performance and does often invoke a sense
of theatricality, which contributes to this confusion. The association of performance with drag and then drag with subversion
in *Gender Trouble* also contributes to the voluntarist interpretation. Nevertheless, as she insists in *Bodies that Matter* (and a
number of other places, e.g. Butler 1988, 1991), the model that
she is employing is not a theatrical model. It is rather a speech
act model based on a poststructuralist understanding of subjectivity. This is a distinction that Butler makes from her very
earliest work and one that she continues to emphasize as she
develops her notion of performativity in later works (Butler
1993a, 1997a, 1997b). It is an important distinction to grasp in
getting to grips with Butler's work in general, and her political
strategies and understanding of social change in particular.

'Performative Acts and Gender Constitution'

Even before the publication of *Gender Trouble*, Butler was
emphasizing the difference between performativity and the

notion of performance in symbolic interactionism, and in phenomenological and ethnomethodological accounts of the enactment of gender, which have been influential in the sociology of gender. In 'Performative Acts and Gender Constitution' (Butler, 1988), she distinguishes between the notion of performance and acts in a performative account of gender and the notions of acts, performances and roles in both the phenomenological approach of Edmund Husserl and Maurice Merleau Ponty, and the symbolic interactionism of George Herbert Mead and Erving Goffman. A significant difference, she argues, lies in the constituting role of the 'doer', or pre-existing self behind these acts. Whereas these earlier accounts seem to imply a 'true self', a 'doer' who is doing the acting, in Butler's notion of performance the 'doer' is produced in and by the act, in a Nietzschean sense, and importantly does not stand outside of, or before it, in a position of reflection. Although she doesn't mention it in this paper, this distinction follows Nietzsche's rejection of the humanist separation of the subject and action. This separation allows the subject to be (mis)taken for the cause of action rather than a product of it.[2]

Therefore, rather than focusing on the ways that 'social agents *constitute* social reality through language, gesture, and all manner of symbolic social sign' (Butler 1988: 519, original emphasis) in the phenomenological tradition, Butler focuses on the 'more radical use of the doctrine of constitution that takes the social agent as an *object* rather than the subject of constitutive acts' (ibid., original emphasis). Furthermore, she argues:

> In opposition to theatrical or phenomenological models which take the gendered self to be prior to its acts, I will understand constituting acts not only as constituting the identity of the actor but as constituting that identity as a compelling illusion, an object of *belief*.
>
> (p. 520, original emphasis)

It is in this sense that gender is 'intentional, non-referential and contingent' as she later claims (Butler 1993a) – even as it is also a constituting aspect of identity and, as such, not a simple matter of volition.

Butler draws on the phenomenological tradition, as work in

this area attempts to provide a theory of embodied subjectivity and human action which does not take the body itself as the source of meaning and identity. It rather focuses on the significatory practices which endow particular bodies with social and symbolic meaning and which structure the everyday actions of embodied subjects. The focus of this approach is thus on 'constituting acts' in the doing of subjectivity rather than on predetermined structures of any sort, or metaphysical questions about the nature of human being that produce the idea of ontologies of gender as substantive features of human being. Indeed, Butler argues that this approach 'moves the conception of gender off the ground of a substantial model of identity to one that requires a conception of a constituted *social temporality*' (Butler 1988: 520, original emphasis).

However, her application of this approach to the performativity of gender involves an extension of the concept of constituting acts beyond the constitution of identity to the constitution of identity as 'a compelling illusion, an object of *belief*' (p. 520, original emphasis), as in the above quote. She wants to get at the ways in which neither sex nor gender is a natural or material fact whose essence can be determined through an examination of physiology or biology and to show that the substantive model of identity is an illusion which is a product of the performance itself. Hence, she draws on 'theatrical, anthropological and philosophical discourses, but mainly phenomenology . . . to show that what is called gender identity is a performative accomplishment compelled by social sanction and taboo' (p. 520). Furthermore: 'In its very character as performative resides the possibility of contesting its reified status' (p. 520).

Butler's attempt to theorize gender as a performance which is performative is therefore far removed from an understanding of gender as a role undertaken by a pre-existing self. It represents a marked departure from, for example, Goffman's account of the performance of roles in the *Presentation of Self in Everyday Life*, 'which posits a self which assumes and exchanges various "roles" within complex social expectations of the "game" of modern life' (p. 528). Butler rejects the very idea of such a self and the view that gender acts are expressive of a core identity, of something prior to the acts themselves that is the cultural, 'spiritual or psychological correlate of a biological sex' (p. 528).[3]

Therefore, as one sociological commentary suggests, despite certain 'echoes', Butler's work is 'somewhat more sophisticated and considerably more complex' than those earlier accounts which draw on the phenomenological tradition (Hood-Williams and Harrison 1998: 84). For one thing, the 'universalistic human subjectivities' which underpin these accounts is displaced in Butler's approach. Hood-Williams and Harrison argue that, unlike Butler, Goffman explicitly bases 'his discussion of gender identity – which is regarded as nothing more than a schedule for its own portrayal – in a general human capacity: the capacity to depict and to read depictions' (p. 83). They also identify similar problems with attempts to draw parallels between Butler's account of gender as performative and the study of gender and transgender in the ethnomethodological tradition that has been very influential in sociology. Garfinkel (1990), for example, described the everyday practicalities of gender interactions in which a pre-operative, male-to-female transsexual, whose name was Agnes, learnt to act like, and so 'become', a woman. He wanted to describe Agnes's styles of speech and the way she communicated as a woman in order to understand the ways in which gendered norms regulate verbal and non-verbal inter-actions. However, his account also rested on a humanist concep-tion of the self (or 'member' to use Garfinkel's own terminology) at the core of identity. Moreover, neither of these approaches was based on a theory of language. Although Goffman gave the example of advertisements as a form of significatory practice to demonstrate that gender is a social performance, rather than an ontological feature of persons (albeit rooted in the human capacity to 'provide and read depictions'), and in this sense at least his account is in keeping with Butler's denaturalization of identity categories. Nevertheless, in Butler's work,

> [g]ender is held to be a significatory practice in which acts are to be understood through linguistic concepts and in which gender subjectivities and identifications are produced and acquire the hardness of gender ontologies in the process of their own reiterated citationality.
>
> (Hood-Williams and Harrison 1998: 84)

These theoretical concerns thus mark a significant difference between Butler's work and the more empirical enquiries of these earlier accounts, as Hood-Williams and Harrison suggest.

Indeed, Butler is not concerned with describing the everyday practicalities of gender interactions in the way that ethnomethodological accounts such as Garfinkel's might, or as in Goffman's symbolic interactionism. On the contrary, her account is criticized precisely because it does not pay attention to these aspects of 'doing' gender (see, for example, Namaste 1996). Moreover, Butler's concern with the constitution of gendered subjectivity involves revealing the ways in which heterosexuality, as a compulsory and unstable regime of power/knowledge, structures the gendered norms that regulate the kind of verbal and nonverbal interactions that Garfinkel and Goffman merely describe.

Hence, the critique of heterosexuality marks a further difference from these earlier sociological enquiries and from the phenomenological tradition more generally, even as it demonstrates the sociological relevance of Butler's work.

This critique also marks a significant difference between Butler's account of gender performativity and the social constructionist models of sex and sexuality that had been developing in sociology and anthropology in the 1960s and 1970s, which also drew on the theoretical perspective of symbolic interactionism, as well as on labelling theory. As Epstein (1996) argues, in these disciplines classic works such as McIntosh (1968) 'The Homosexual Role', and later Plummer (1975) and Weeks (1977) paved the way for the growth of gay and lesbian studies and queer theory in the 1980s and 1990s. However, although it involved a rejection of essentialist understandings of sexuality, including homosexuality, whether in biological or psychological terms, it too tended to focus on sexual identities and meanings as a matter of inter-subjective negotiation. Hence, although these earlier sociological approaches provided a welcome corrective to pathological models of homosexuality and psychologistic explanations of homosexual behaviour (Namaste 1996),[4] they tended to focus on the social organization of homosexual behaviour and identity as marginal rather than 'the centrality of marginality' (Epstein 1996: 147) to the wider organization of society and culture. This is clearly a significant aspect of Butler's critique of heterosexuality as a regime of power/knowledge.

Indeed, the theoretical concern with heterosexuality as a

regime of power/knowledge also provides an early indication of Butler's controversial understanding of the way to effect change in social relations. As she explains in 'Performative Acts and Gender Constitution', the problem with sociological or pheno-menological accounts that start with constituting acts as a 'theoretical point of departure' is that this doesn't allow atten-tion to the 'scale and systemic character of women's oppression' (Butler 1988: 525). Whilst such individual acts might be necessary to the continuation of inequalities and oppression, 'it doesn't follow that oppression is a sole consequence of such acts' (p. 525).

> The transformation of social relations becomes a matter, then, of transforming hegemonic social conditions rather than the individual acts that are spawned by these condi-tions. Indeed, one runs the risk of addressing the merely indirect if not epiphenomenal, reflection of those conditions if one remains restricted to a politics of acts.
>
> (p. 525)

The problem of how precisely to transform those hegemonic social relations, as well as how to identify the form they take and the ways they work in the constitution of subjectivity, occu-pies much of Butler's subsequent work. In *Gender Trouble* and *Bodies that Matter*, it becomes a matter of the subversion of identity and the displacement of the 'heterosexual matrix' or 'heterosexual hegemony', which are discussed below and in Chapter 2. However, before moving on to Butler's critique of heterosexuality as a regime of power/knowledge and the possi-bilities for social change that this implies, let me return for a moment to Butler's account of performativity in *Gender Trouble* and the ways in which gender can usefully be thought of in terms of performances and acts, and how this relates to the body.

'In what senses, then, is gender an act?'[5]

Gender, then, is an act in the sense that 'doing' gender involves 'sustained social performances' which involve the repetition of socially established meanings. It is also an act in the sense that 'gender attributes and acts [are] the various ways in which a body shows or produces its cultural signification' (Butler 1990a: 141). In so doing, such acts effectively constitute the identity they would seem to merely express, or reveal.

In other words, gender acts are what constitute embodied beings as gendered subjects in keeping with the norms of compulsory heterosexuality. They involve an on-going process of continual repetition ('sustained social performances') through which individual subjects do (act out) their gender, in a 'stylized repetition of acts'. This 'stylized repetition of acts' involves bodily movements and gestures (corporeal styles) that are socially approved and politically regulated in keeping with 'a cultural field of gender hierarchy and compulsory heterosexuality' (p. 139). The enactment of gender is thus socially approved and politically regulated rather than dictated by some kind of internal nature.

Indeed, far from being an internal property of a pre-existing subject, a stable identity or source of agency as in a metaphysics of substance, gender is rather tenuously constituted in time through this 'stylized repetition of acts'. It is through this that the illusion of a stable fixed identity is promoted, perpetuated and believed. Butler is using the notion of 'style' in the combined sense of Sartre's 'a style of being', Foucault's 'stylistics of existence', and de Beauvoir's view of bodies as 'styles of the flesh' to get at the way in which gender is a kind of 'corporeal enactment'. Furthermore, she emphasizes that 'these styles are never fully self-styled, for styles have a history and those histories condition and limit the possibilities' (p. 139). Therefore, although the body plays a vital role in all this, it is not as in the naturalistic fallacy; that the gendered body is performative 'suggests it has no ontological status apart from the various acts which constitute its reality' (p. 136). It is rather in the Foucauldian sense of a 'surface politics of the body' in *Gender Trouble*. Hence, gender becomes 'an enacted fantasy or incorporation' in which acts, gestures and desires produce the effect of an internal core or substance, but produce this on the surface of the body. 'Such acts, gestures, enactments, generally construed, are *performative* in the sense that the essence or identity that they otherwise purport to express are *fabrications*, manufactured and sustained through corporeal signs and other discursive means' (p. 136, original emphasis). In other words, these 'acts and gestures, articulated and enacted desires create the illusion of an interior and organizing gender core, an illusion discursively maintained for the purposes of the regulation of sexuality within the obligatory frame of reproductive heterosexuality' (p. 136). This makes it seem as if the 'cause' of these acts, gender and desire, lie within the self. It also masks from view the ways in which they are politically regulated products of disciplinary practices that work to sustain compulsory heterosexuality and gender hierarchy; and the ways in which compulsory heterosexuality compels the kind of gender practices through which it is sustained, along with the belief in its naturalness. Butler argues that the fact that people who act outside of appropriate gender norms are policed and punished is evidence of this. Furthermore, she argues:

> Because there is neither an 'essence' that gender expresses or externalises nor an objective ideal to which gender aspires, and because gender is not a fact, the various acts of gender create the idea of gender, and without those acts, there would be no gender at all.
>
> (p. 140)

Gender, then, is a matter of the repetition of gender acts in which all aspects, including any sense of a psychological interiority, are fictional products of reproductive heterosexuality.[6] And reproductive heterosexuality is also a fictional construct, which works as a regulatory ideal in Butler's account of performativity.

Performance, imitation and drag: the critique of heterosexuality

In her critical genealogies in *Gender Trouble*, Butler draws on the insights of gay and lesbian sexuality and same-sex desire to demonstrate that heterosexuality is an ideal, a 'regulatory fiction'. She argues that it is exposed as such by discontinuities in lesbian, gay, bisexual and heterosexual contexts, in which gender does not necessarily follow from sex, and desire and sexuality do not seem to follow from gender. However, the disciplinary production of gender creates a false stabilization and coherence in the interests of reproductive heterosexuality. This works to conceal the discontinuities which undermine the model of gender identity as expressing an inner core. When these are taken into account, 'the regulatory ideal is then exposed as a norm and a fiction that disguises itself as a developmental law regulating the sexual field that it purports to describe' (Butler 1990a: 136). She wants to show that contrary to popular belief, heterosexuality is not so much a natural result of a biological sex or sexed nature, as a fictional ideal that regulates the production of sexed subjects and identities.

Butler draws on the work of Monique Wittig, who argues that sex is a political category. Although she disagrees with some aspects of Wittig's 'materialist' approach, she nevertheless argues that there are aspects of it that are in keeping with her account of the performativity of gender.[7] Thus she cites her approvingly:

> A materialist feminist approach shows that what we take for the cause or origin of oppression is in fact only the *mark* imposed by the oppressor . . . what we believe to be a physical and direct perception is only a sophisticated and mythic construction, an 'imaginary formation'.
>
> (Wittig cited in Butler 1990a: 25, original emphasis)

What Butler takes from this approach then is the idea that sex is a political category which works to found society as heterosexual. This involves the view that the binary restriction on sex, and the understanding of sexual difference as essential, serve the interests of reproductive heterosexuality as a compulsory system. It also involves the idea that bodies are culturally constituted and Butler takes from Wittig's view of this the idea that 'morphology itself is a consequence of a hegemonic conceptual scheme' (p. xii), i.e. reproductive heterosexuality. (Indeed, Butler builds on this view of morphology in her critique of the Lacanian symbolic order in *Bodies that Matter*, which is discussed in Chapter 2.)

However, Butler disagrees with Wittig's account in a number of important ways, all of which relate to her commitment to poststructuralism. She doesn't agree with Wittig's focus on gender practices and institutions, such as the patriarchal family, as the material *grounds* of heterosexist oppression, or her view of language as merely a tool with which to express it. For Butler, the focus is on the production of meaning itself, in and through these concrete practices, rather than seeing them as the material roots of it. Hence, her focus is on the materiality of signs and signification, and heterosexuality as a regulatory ideal and conceptual (epistemic and ontological) regime. For Butler, the institutions and practices that Wittig takes as the material grounds of heterosexual oppression are rather material *consequences* of such conceptual schemes. Butler also rejects Wittig's view of gay and lesbian sexuality as outside of, and radically 'other' to, heterosexuality and thus free of heterosexual norms. She also rejects Wittig's rather controversial view that since women and men are products of heterosexual social relations, rather than biology or nature, stepping outside of those social relations, as lesbians do, means that lesbians are not women. In addition to these differences, and implicated in all of them, Butler rejects Wittig's humanist view of the subject. Hence: 'Wittig calls for a position beyond sex that returns her theory to a problematic humanism based in a problematic metaphysics of presence' (p. 124).

This reference to the 'metaphysics of presence' refers to Derrida's poststructuralist development of Nietzsche's critique of the metaphysics of substance. In Derrida's view, the metaphysics of presence is a fundamental feature of Western thought and culture and the mainstay of the modern philosophical tradition. At its most basic, it involves the idea that we can have pure, unmediated knowledge of the world and the subjects in it. It also involves the logic of non-contradiction, in which identity and certainty are privileged through the suppression of difference and ambiguity.[8] This 'myth of presence' underpins the humanist view of the subject, as the unified, rational 'I', who can transcend nature and culture; who can observe the world objectively in the pursuit of universal truth. Derrida's deconstructive strategies aim to demonstrate the impossibility of presence and access to an independent reality, or humanist subject, outside of our conceptual schemes. His deconstruction of many canonical philosophical texts highlights the exclusions that are required for the illusion of presence (and Western humanism) to be maintained. Butler's critique of Wittig is that she does seem to presume this kind of presence in her call for a move beyond 'sex', even though she also seems to challenge the metaphysics of substance in her critique of the cultural construction of sex, gender and the body. She also seems to assume this kind of presence in her reliance on a humanist subject 'as the metaphysical locus of agency' (p. 25). In addition, Wittig's assumption of a position beyond sex misses the ways in which what is excluded from identity is nevertheless in a sense required for its construction. Where Derrida's critique of presence aims to demonstrate this paradoxical feature of identity in relation to the exclusions on which the Western philosophical tradition is based, Butler aims to demonstrate it in relation to the performativity of gender identity, and the exclusions involved in the maintenance of heterosexual hegemony. Although this debt to Derrida is not made fully explicit in *Gender Trouble*, the critique of presence and of *différance* (which is discussed below), is a pervasive influence in her account of performativity.

Thus Butler argues with Wittig, and some aspects of psychoanalysis, that lesbian and gay perspectives on sex and sexuality suggest that the idea of a coherent heterosexuality is a normative ideal, and that it involves sexual positions that are intrinsically impossible to embody. However, in contrast to Wittig and, I would argue, more in keeping with Derrida's critique of presence, Butler argues that these perspectives suggest that heterosexuality is not only a compulsory system, but is 'an intrinsic comedy, a constant parody of itself' (p. 122).

In *Gender Trouble* (and in Butler 1991) she develops the idea of heterosexuality as involving parody and imitation by drawing an analogy between gender acts and drag acts, based on Esther Newton's (1972) anthropological account of drag artists. This account suggests that 'drag is not an imitation or a copy of some prior and true gender; according to Newton, drag enacts the very structure of impersonation by which any gender is assumed' (1991: 28). Butler thus takes from Newton the suggestion that the structure of impersonation is an important mechanism in the social construction of gender. She argues: 'In imitating gender, drag implicitly reveals the imitative structure of gender itself' (Butler 1990a: 137). Rather than being a foundational category based on the reality of heterosexuality, gender becomes 'a kind of persistent impersonation that passes as the real' (p. viii). Moreover, that this view of imitation and gender parody does not imply an original is of particular significance for Butler: 'The parody is *of* the very notion of an original . . . To be more precise it is a product which, in effect – that is in its effects – postures as an imitation' (p. 138, original emphasis). Hence, against the view in some feminist theories that drag acts and some aspects of gay and lesbian relationships, such as butch/ femme, imitate stereotypical heterosexual relations, Butler argues that they rather demonstrate that the very idea of an original heterosexuality is a myth. She also suggests, in Nietzschean fashion, that 'laughter emerges in the realization that all along the original was derived' (p. 139).

Parody, politics and subversion

The significance of all this for Butler is that heterosexuality is both compulsory and fundamentally unstable. Unstable, as Deutscher puts it, 'because of the perpetual need for reiteration and re-enactment because parody lies at the heart of "natural" gender' (Deutscher 1997: 26). Compulsory in the sense that 'acting out of line with heterosexual norms brings with it ostracism, punishment, and violence, not to mention the transgressive pleasures produced by those very prohibitions' (Butler 1991: 24). This then 'can become an occasion for a subversive and proliferating parody of gender norms in which the very claim to originality and to the real is shown to be the effect of a certain kind of naturalized gender mime' (p. 23). Furthermore, '[t]his perpetual displacement constitutes a fluidity of identities that suggests an openness to resignification and recontextualization: parodic proliferation deprives hegemonic culture and its critics of the claim to naturalized or essentialist gender identities' (p. 138).

Thus Butler associates the denaturalization of heterosexist gender categories with instability and the *possibility* of subversion and resignification. As mentioned earlier, her stated aims in *Gender Trouble* were not only to denaturalize but also to *destabilize* identity categories such as sex, gender, desire and the body and the epistemic ontological regime that produced them. Thus she claims:

As a strategy to denaturalize and resignify bodily categories,

I describe and propose a set of parodic practices based in a performative theory of gender acts that disrupt the categories of the body, sex, gender and sexuality and occasion their subversive resignification and proliferation beyond the binary frame.

(Butler, 1990a: xii)

However, this claim has attracted much criticism. Indeed, the whole question of parody as politics and subversion has proved very problematic. Not least in that this view of gender as an imitation for which there is no original, or 'real', foundation seems to imply that gender is a mere artifice that can be changed at will; and describing the perpetual displacement involved as constituting a 'fluidity of identities' also seems to suggest this. Although Butler attempts to address this in *Bodies that Matter*, and she further develops an account of the intractability of gender categories in the *Psychic Life of Power* (discussed in Chapter 3), the issue of subversion continues to be a problematic aspect of her work for many commentators and activists who draw on her work. One of the main reasons for this is precisely because her account of performativity involves neither voluntarism nor a humanist view of the subject as a source of agency that a voluntarist account would involve. How can there be resistance and change to dominant social relations if there is no such subject underneath or outside them? Where does resistance come from if there is no 'doer behind the deed'? Or, as Alison Assiter puts it, voicing the concerns of many feminist critics: 'How can one create oneself as a self if there is no antecedently existing self to do the creating?' and 'How can we create a feminist politics that deconstructs the female subject?' (Assiter 1996: 10).

However, Butler isn't so much suggesting that we can *freely* create ourselves so much as identifying the multiplicity of mechanisms through which we are created, and highlighting the ways these work to conceal that fact, and trying to identify the potential for change within this. From the perspective of performativity, we simply cannot create ourselves as ourselves in an unmediated sense. Feminist politics needs to recognize this rather than focusing on the apparently debilitating aspects of the deconstruction of the category woman. Since we are products of discourses, language and significations that structure the acts in which we engage and through which we are constituted as subjects, and as ourselves, what we can do is to aim at alternative significations in the course of our repetition of these acts. Since compulsory heterosexuality and phallogocentrism as epistemological and ontological regimes are significant sources of the acts which constitute gendered embodiment, the route to change in this area is through repetitions that subvert dominant gender norms in the hope of destabilizing and displacing these regimes.

However, although *Gender Trouble* has been interpreted in the main as arguing for the proliferation of drag performances in a politics of parody as particularly subversive of gender norms, quite how this destabilization is to be effected and how subversive this is as a strategy is not at all clear. Deutscher, for instance, suggests that: 'Butler is not discussing subversion as political strategy, but rather as something which lies at the heart of all reproducibility' (Deutscher 1997: 26). Gender norms are enabled by their own internal instability, by the necessity of reproducibility and parody. Nevertheless, she points out, for Butler 'the enabling function of parody retains some kind of *promise* as subversive . . . Parody shows that gender norms are not stable. Parody opens up, she will say, the possibility for new configurations' (p. 27, original emphasis). However, there is some ambiguity here, as Deutscher argues, as Butler sometimes also seems to close down the association between parody and subversion, suggesting rather that parody would result simply in a 'temporary and futile disruption of the hegemony of the paternal law' (p. 26, citing Butler 1990a: 81).

Indeed, Butler herself goes on to argue in *Bodies that Matter* that drag is not necessarily subversive. Moreover, in Butler (1994a) she insists that although in *Gender Trouble* she aims at discursive resignifications through a politics of gender parody and drag, drag is offered nevertheless as an example of performativity not as the paradigm of performativity that it is often taken to be. Thus she comments in *Bodies that Matter*:

> As *Paris is Burning* made clear drag is not unproblematically subversive. It serves a subversive function to the extent that it reflects the mundane impersonations by which hetero-

sexually ideal genders are performed and naturalized and undermines their power by virtue of effecting that exposure. But there is no guarantee that exposing the naturalized status of heterosexuality will lead to its subversion. Heterosexuality can augment its hegemony through its denaturalization, as when we see denaturalizing parodies that reidealize heterosexual norms without calling them into question.

(Butler 1993a: 231)

Nevertheless her point is still that it can be subversive, enabling social and political resignifications. As she says in an interview in *Radical Philosophy* in 1994: 'we don't know when resistance is going to be recouped or when it will be groundbreaking. It's like breaking through to a new set of paradigms' (Butler 1994a: 38). Moreover, in typical Foucauldian vein, she argues that this is but one site of struggle amongst others.

Despite Butler's own optimism then, this view of resistance and change through subversive repetition has not only proved problematic for many feminist critics, but it has also generated much misunderstanding about the 'nature' of gender, agency and change in Butler's work. Moreover her attempt to explain it in *Gender Trouble*, through the example of drag, has probably raised more problems than it has solved. Indeed, despite her attempts to address the issue of resistance and change in subsequent work, as she develops her account of performativity, it remains an intractable problem for many commentators. As such, it will be discussed again in later chapters, especially Chapter 2, in relation to feminist politics, and Chapter 5, in relation to trans politics. However, for now I want to continue with the issue of how Butler's account of resistance and change could be said to involve a notion of active agency, and how the subject could be a source of resistance if there is no 'doer behind the deed'.

The constituted subject and the possibility of agency

Basically, Butler is arguing that gender and gender identities are constructed through relations of power that are inherent in normative constraints that involve the sedimentation of gender norms over time. This isn't a founding constitution however that takes place once and for all; it involves a continuous process of 'ritualized repetition'. Since it is through this process that bodily beings, in all their diversity, are produced and regulated, the necessary repetition involved provides both the space and the possibility for change. What is required is a critical reworking of those gender norms. In *Gender Trouble* this takes the form of a politics of parody, cross dressing etc. The notion of performativity is developed in *Bodies that Matter* (Butler 1993a) and later *Excitable Speech* (Butler 1997a) by placing more emphasis on speech act theory to show how discourses constitute subjectivity, and that this involves a continual process of citation and recitation that provides the possibility for change without an intentional subject who can stand outside of this process. These developments are discussed in Chapters 3 and 4 respectively. For now, suffice it to say that although performativity consists of the reiteration of norms which 'precede, constrain and exceed the performer . . . further what is "performed" works to conceal, if not to disavow, what remains opaque, unconscious unperformable' (Butler 1993a: 234), Butler still wants to argue that it is the open-ended process of repetition and recitation that provides the conditions of possibility for subversive repetitions and thus agency. Although in this account of performativity 'we' as subjects cannot be separated from the discursive conventions through which we are constituted, the possibility of opposing and reworking them is crucial to it.

Precisely because the 'doer' is not an intentional subject who stands behind the act as its originator, but is rather constituted within it, as Butler insists in *Feminist Contentions*: 'the "doer" will be the uncertain working of the discursive possibilities by which it itself is worked' (Butler 1995a: 135).

To put it another way, Butler's account of performativity is an attempt to theorize subjectivity in a way that locates the formation of the subject in history and culture, rejecting the notion of the universal, transcendental subject, and the gender hierarchy on which it is based. However, it is not merely that subjects are embedded in history and culture, but rather the stronger claim that the subject is historically and culturally constituted. The 'I' that is presumed to be the origin and cause of action, and the foundation of knowledge, thus becomes a historical effect. Whilst not being reducible to a mere linguistic product, this 'I', as Butler puts it, is nevertheless linguistically instituted. It is not that the 'I' itself is situated prior to discourse, which then gives it a means of expression. It is rather that the discursive constitution of the 'I' precedes any particular 'I', as its 'transitive invocation'. 'The "I" is thus a citation of the place of the "I" in speech' (Butler 1993a: 226). Moreover, 'that place has a certain priority and anonymity with respect to the life it animates: it is the historically revisable possibility of a name that precedes and exceeds me, but without which I cannot speak' (p. 226). And it is these conditions and this historical revisability that provide the possibility for agency and change.

It is also because of this possibility that Butler argues that her account of subjectivity as constituted in this way does not involve rejecting altogether the idea of subjectivity and agency, or critique and historical change, which is often argued are the necessary correlates of the 'death' of the universal, transcendental subject in its strong form (e.g. Benhabib 1992; Benhabib *et al.* 1995). Although it involves a rejection of a humanist choosing subject who can stand outside of history and culture and reflect on it, and a view of gender identity as socially constructed, Butler also wants to reject cultural determinism and to retain a view of gender practices as sites of change, or as she puts it herself, 'critical agency'. Nevertheless, both agency and critique are clearly reconceived.

Critique

Butler explains her position on the possibility of agency and critique in *Feminist Contentions*, where she debates the significance of many of the issues involved with Seyla Benhabib, Drucilla Cornell and Nancy Fraser (Benhabib *et al.* 1995). One of the thorny problems under debate concerns the issue of how agency could be possible without the existence of a humanist subject (an 'intentional doer behind the deed'). This also raises the problem of how the grounds for 'critique' could be possible without any foundation in such a subject.

Butler says that she would not use the term 'critique' in this way because the idea of grounds is suggestive of the very foundationalism that her account of performativity aims to avoid.[9] Her concern in this is with the power regimes that constitute us, the particular discourses and performative acts through which we achieve subjectivity. These are historically specific. They are the concrete conditions under which agency becomes possible, even though there is no possibility of getting outside of them to some essential self untainted by them. In answering Benhabib's criticisms of her view of agency, Butler makes the following point which is particularly illuminating:

> I would argue that there is no possibility of standing outside of the discursive conventions by which we are enabled. Gender performativity is not a question of instrumentally deploying a 'masquerade', for such a construal of performativity presupposes an intentional subject behind the deed. On the contrary, gender performativity involves the difficult labour of deriving agency from the very power regimes which constitute us, and which we oppose. This is, oddly enough, historical work, reworking the historicity of the signifier, and no recourse to quasi-transcendental selfhood and inflated concepts of History will help us in this most concrete and paradoxical of struggles.
>
> (Butler 1995a: 136)

According to Butler therefore, critique is immanent to particular discursive regimes and 'the practice of "critique" is implicated in the very power-relations it seeks to adjudicate' (p. 138).

Agency

Agency then is not something that is presupposed in the structure of a prediscursive, universal self and as such prior to power and language.[10] '[I]f the subject is a reworking of the very discursive processes by which it is worked then "agency" is to be found the possibilities of signification opened up by discourse' (p. 135). Or, as she puts it in *Gender Trouble*, since 'the substantive "I" only appears through a signifying practice that seeks to conceal its own workings and to naturalize its effects the question of agency is reformulated as a question of how signification and resignification work' (Butler 1990a: 144). Discourse thus becomes the 'horizon of agency' and performativity becomes a matter of signification. Conceiving of agency in this way means that it becomes a contingent possibility that is the effect of historically specific discursive conditions and power relations. Just as Butler's notion of performance and performativity avoids metaphysical questions about the ontological status of sexual difference because it focuses on the way that sexual difference functions as ontological difference, in the contemporary epistemic/ontological regime. This view of agency does not involve metaphysical questions about the self, it rather involves an investigation of the concrete conditions under which agency becomes possible (Butler 1995a).

However, the understanding of 'concrete conditions' implied here has proved rather problematic for many feminist commentators because these are considered to be a matter of signification and resignification. Furthermore, Butler's insistence that agency is 'a contingent possibility that is the effect of historically specific discursive conditions and power relations' is also problematic. For one thing, as it is contingent, it isn't necessary, and so how can we tell when it is there and when it is not? This would seem to be a crucial question for those whose aim is to effect social change, yet Butler's account does not provide a means of addressing this question. Additionally, the 'historically specific discursive conditions and power relations' that she refers to also become a matter of the workings of signification in her account, not something that exists outside of it as in, say, a materialist account such as Jackson's, Ebert's or for that matter Wittig's, which was discussed earlier. From the perspective of performativity, the concrete material reality which these accounts would argue that Butler neglects (e.g. gender relations, the patriarchal family, the female body) can't be the starting point of feminist analysis because they are not independent of the workings of signification and resignification but rather products of it. The account of performativity is a means of highlighting the ways in which this works.

Hence the question of how signification and resignification work is a crucial aspect of Butler's account of agency. It is through this that she aims to show how it is that to be *constituted* by discourse is not necessarily the same as to be *determined* by discourse. Already, in *Gender Trouble* she argues that:

The subject is not *determined* by the rules through which it is generated because signification is *not a founding act, but rather a regulated process of repetition* that both conceals itself and enforces its rules precisely through the production of substantializing effects.

(Butler 1990a: 145, original emphasis)

Moreover, she continues, 'it is only *within* the practices of repetitive signifying that a subversion of identity becomes possible' (p. 145).

However, the question of how signification and resignification work is not fully resolved in *Gender Trouble*. Her suggestions there regarding the subversion of identity are also problematic, as already discussed, and her notion of agency is underdeveloped. In *Bodies that Matter* she develops the notion of temporality involved in the performativity of gender in a way that that helps to develop these areas. In *Gender Trouble* the inherent repeatability of gender acts is already emphasized, but in *Bodies that Matter* she draws on Derrida's notion of iterability to develop an account of the performativity of gender that involves a notion of historicity, and the iteration and reiteration of norms, or 'citational practices' in ways are more clearly open to change. Moreover in *The Psychic Life of Power* (1997b) she develops these ideas to argue that power is not something that is simply external to the subject, or wielded by a subject, it is rather something that works on and through subjects in a process of reiteration. Thus: '[I]f conditions of power are to persist, they must be reiterated: the subject is precisely the site of such reiteration, a reiteration that is never merely mechanical' (p. 16). Crucially, then, although the subject therefore may be the site of the reiteration of the conditions of power in the form of significatory practices, such reiterations are not merely mechanical. This is because the reiteration of power not only temporalizes the conditions of subordination but renders them 'active and productive' rather than static.

This ambivalence, which she describes as a 'reiterated ambivalence at the heart of agency' (p. 18) provides the conditions for the possibility of change. However, it does not guarantee change nor is it something that can be rendered unambivalent. Nevertheless, Butler wants to embrace this insight with a certain amount of optimism. She argues that although agency is implicated in subordination (as discussed in Chapter 3), this 'is not the sign of a fatal self-contradiction at the core of the subject and, hence, further proof of its pernicious or obsolete character' (p. 17). It does mean, however, that the question of agency becomes a question of 'how to take an oppositional relation to power that is, admittedly, implicated in the very power one opposes' (p. 17).

This is a question that continued to haunt Foucault's work. Butler tries to avoid some of the limitations of his work. In particular, the failure to reconcile theoretically the possibility of resistance with his depiction of the body, sex and subjectivity as discursive effects, despite his insistence that there is no power without resistance. Foucault himself was aware of these difficulties. Indeed, perhaps because of them, he switched his attention from the body/subject to the problematic of the self in his later works, where he attempted to formulate an 'aesthetics of existence', leaving various problems in this area unanswered. Drawing on Derrida's work concerning the nature of the performative, in particular iterability, temporality and citationality, allows Butler to retain the notion of sex and gender as discursive effects, whilst avoiding the ultimate determinism of Foucault's account by opening up the space for resistance and change as discussed below (and again in Chapters 3 and 4). She says she wants to avoid the 'political fatalism' of those who would discount the possibility of agency in a constituted subject and the 'naive political optimism' (p. 16) of those who would cling to the classical liberal-humanist notion of subjectivity.

This turn to Derrida also helps to shed light on other related criticisms of Butler's account of performativity, in particular the critique of binary oppositions and the suggestion that her account retains a monolithic account of gender.

Critique of binary oppositions

The critique of binary oppositions is an important element in Butler's account of performativity in *Gender Trouble* and *Bodies that Matter*. Indeed, the attempt to avoid binary thinking is proving a somewhat intractable problem for many contemporary feminist theorists concerned with the body and sexual difference, and it is argued that despite an expressed attempt to avoid it, Butler does not manage to do so. One such criticism is that Butler employs a dualistic logic of inclusion/exclusion, domination/resistance that is inimical to a move beyond binary thinking and ultimately results in the retention of a monolithic notion of gender. Another involves the claim that her account of performativity ultimately retains a representation/ matter dichotomy.

McNay (1999) argues that although Butler wants to develop a dynamic and non-dichotomous model of the body and identity in *Gender Trouble* and *Bodies that Matter*, through an emphasis on the instability of dominant norms and the openness involved in the production of identity, her account in fact continues dichotomous thinking rather than breaking with it. Furthermore, despite Butler's insights concerning the constitutive instability of heterosexuality and 'dominant norms', her concept of normative gender identity remains monolithic. McNay argues that this results from the notion of temporality which Butler employs. She sees Butler's notion of performativity as relying 'predominantly on a version of the Freudian idea of repetition compulsion and as such reactive and according to some an atemporal concept' (McNay cites Smith 1996). Thus:

> This emphasis on the retrospective dimensions of time – the performative as 'a repetition, a sedimentation, a congealment of the past' (Butler 1993a: 244) – leads to an overemphasis on the internal uniformity of gender norms. Reiteration becomes a static rather than temporal act where the reproduction of the sex/gender system involves a ceaseless reinscription of the same. This notion of time as a succession of self-identical and discrete acts renders the dominant hermetic and self-sustaining – it emphasises the uniformity of gender norms, for example – and means that disruption can only come from outside. This provokes the dualisms of subjection–resistance, exclusion–inclusion that limit Butler's work.
>
> (McNay 1999: 102)

However, as I have tried to show, Butler tries to avoid this notion of temporality and in a footnote in *Bodies that Matter*, she makes it clear that this is not the notion of temporality that she wants to employ (Butler 1993a: 244). She explains that she is drawing on a Derridean notion of temporality, and comments on the significance of this for the notion of iterability. Thus:

> As a sedimented effect of reiterative or ritual practice, sex acquires its naturalized effect, and yet, it is also by virtue of this reiteration that gaps and fissures are opened up as the constitutive instabilities in such constructions, as that which escapes or exceeds the norm, as that which cannot be wholly defined or fixed by the repetitive labor of that norm.
>
> (Butler 1993a: 10)

Reiteration is a sedimented process but, to reiterate, it is not a mechanical process. It needs to be thought in the context of Derrida's account of the performativity of language and iterability, and of excess, as in his notion of dissemination, as that which cannot be captured by representation.

Derrida's notion of dissemination also helps to shed light on the claim that Butler's account of signification ultimately retains a representation/matter dichotomy. Bray and Colebrook argue that:

> Butler's challenging discursive critique of sex still posits a duality between signification and matter, where matter is seen as radically anterior. Representation would always remain in some sense a negation of matter – a break with a prior materiality, even where that materiality is an effect of representation. Instead of thinking of the body and matter as already coterminous within a general discursive field, Butler's reading posits the body, or matter, as an originary effect of discursive repression.
>
> (Bray and Colebrook 1998: 44–5)

Hence Bray and Colebrook argue that although Butler's account of the performativity of sex and gender serves to complicate dualism, it does not succeed in overcoming it because it involves a view of representation as a negation of corporeality. However, I would argue that Butler's notion of performativity does not involve a view of language and signification that relies on either a representation/matter duality or a negation of corporeality.

The excess to representation that Butler conceives is better understood in terms of Derrida's notion of dissemination as something inaccessible, spilling over; some other to representation in the sense of 'more than', rather than as produced through a dichotomy between matter and representation. In terms of the body, this means that it is not that there is a body that then comes to be represented, but rather that we can only 'know' the body in and through the system of representation and associated norms which produces or constitutes it. It is not therefore a question of a prior body that is then negated. To make this clearer, it is necessary to dwell a little longer on Butler's debt to Derrida's notion of representation as about 'force and signification'.

Derrida and the failure of the performative

Like Derrida, Butler does not assume a permanent structure of exclusion, or a fixed outside to signification. She rather aims to accommodate the contingent cultural and historical aspects of sexed and gendered identity with the fact that sexed identifications are also in some way compelling. It is for this reason that she adds Derrida's reworking of speech act theory to the Foucauldian notion of power as she develops her account of the her notion of the performativity of sex in *Bodies that Matter* (rather than gender as in *Gender Trouble*), as discussed in Chapter 2. Of particular concern is the connection between the norm and the failure of signification in Derrida's notion of performativity. This is because for Derrida the failure of signification is revealed to be intrinsic to the law of the performative rather than an accidental aspect, precisely because of the incompleteness of language.[11] (This is explained in more detail in Chapter 2.)

Butler applies these insights to her concern with the compulsory character of heterosexuality. Hence, as Ziarek puts it: 'It is precisely because iterability fails to perpetuate the identical and pure form of the law that any identity claims have to be reinforced by exclusions – they require "a constitutive outside" ' (Ziarek 1997: 129). This brings us back to the disagreement with Wittig. In this formulation, the process of exclusion performs a normative and normalizing function. In *Bodies that Matter*, 'the constitutive outside' becomes a social abject whose exclusion ensures the domain of social intelligibility (which is also discussed in Chapter 2).

The normativity of heterosexuality thus depends on, and works through, the production of these exclusions. The importance of this, as Ziarek rightly suggests, is that the exclusions that constitute this excluded realm, the social abject, are thus rendered unstable, historical and contingent rather than being seen as an ahistorical Real, in a Lacanian sense. That which is excluded is not conceived as some sort of pre-discursive entity, therefore, but rather 'those possibilities of signification that threaten the purity and permanence of the law instituting sexual difference' (Ziarek 1997: 129). Moreover, conceiving of these exclusions in terms of the abject in this way enables Butler to move beyond the limitations of the Lacanian notion of the symbolic and imaginary which renders sexual difference immutable. It is rather a case of calling into question the fixity of sexual difference through 'the disruptive return of the excluded from within the very logic of the heterosexual symbolic' (Butler 1993a: 12). Indeed, one of the main concerns of *Bodies that Matter* is to 'pursue the possibility of such disruption' (p. 12).

This is discussed in Chapter 2, but for now the point is that as Butler develops these insights within an explicitly Foucauldian notion of discourse and the discursive constitution of reality, the inside/outside, inclusion/exclusion dichotomies are productions within discourse. They do not involve a radically anterior corporeality that is already marked by sexual difference as in certain other feminist theories of the body. These exclusions, Butler emphasizes, are productions within discourse and provide the conditions of possibility for particular dominant discourses such as compulsory heterosexuality. Her account of the materialization of bodies, in *Bodies that Matter* (which is also discussed in Chapter 2), involves a notion of reiterated and reiterable regulatory power in the Foucauldian sense that it is productive, as well as controlling, and that it works in a normative way to produce embodied subjects. And one of the effects of this power is the production of an outside – in this sense abjected, unintelligible bodies that serve as the 'constitutive conditions' for the domain of intelligible bodies. Hence her aim in *Bodies that Matter*:

to understand how what has been foreclosed or banished from the proper domain of 'sex' – where that domain is secured through a heterosexualizing imperative – might at once be produced as a troubling return, not only as an imaginary contestation that effects a failure in the workings of the inevitable law, but as an enabling disruption, the occasion for a radical rearticulation of the symbolic horizon in which bodies come to matter at all.

(p. 23)

In *The Psychic Life of Power* more attention is paid to the psychic aspects of these exclusions and their role in the formation of 'stubborn attachments', as discussed in Chapter 3. To return to McNay's argument for a moment, when considered in these contexts it becomes clear that this is not a static model of domination or performativity. The sedimentations and congealments referred to in *Gender Trouble* and elsewhere are not passed on in a uniform manner precisely because of the failure of signification, which is also and simultaneously the failure of the performative. Moreover, Butler is not presenting the possibilities for change in terms of a Foucauldian reverse discourse but rather in psychoanalytic terms of disruption or the return of the repressed (as I demonstrate in Chapter 2). A significant difference is that for Lacan, what is excluded can only return at the price of psychosis, whereas in Butler's notion of performativity, her understanding of the historicity of the symbolic framework and sexual difference avoids this. Therefore, I would argue that the logic of inclusion/exclusion that McNay regards as a weakness in Butler's work is rather a strength.

As for the claim that Butler's account of performativity in *Gender Trouble* and *Bodies that Matter* involves a monolithic view of gender, this finds resonance with other critics who claim that it reduces everything to sex, and with Hood-Williams and Harrison's suggestion that it displays certain universalizing tendencies. The suggestion here is that Butler's account risks replacing ontological theories of gender with 'an equally foundationalist conception of gender performativity' (Hood-Williams and Harrison 1998: 88). Furthermore, the emphasis on 'heterosexual imperatives and heterosexual hegemony can easily substitute for earlier universalistic deployments of the concept of patriarchy' (p. 88). Plus, they claim in relation to her account of the materialization of the body that 'sex, even when characterized as "sex", has no monopoly on the materialization of bodies which occurs in a range of registers' (pp. 90–1).

Although the materialization of the body is the topic of the next chapter, I would argue that what Butler's account shows is that whilst this latter point may well be true, the categories of sex and gender are, nevertheless, present in *every* scene, but working in conjunction with each of those other registers and in the context of heterosexual hegemony, in particular historical and cultural contexts. As such, neither sex nor gender is monolithic as this would imply a certain uniformity, that very uniformity that Butler's critique of identity categories aims to undermine. It is rather that they are shown to be significant aspects of the social production of persons within particular historical contexts. Indeed, this understanding does not involve the kind of universals that are often deemed necessary to feminist politics and, in some feminist theories of the body (that are discussed in Chapter 2), precisely because for Butler, any always and everywhere aspects are particular products of the regimes that constitute us, rather than essential attributes of the persons who are so constituted. The social performances that constitute gendered persons are thus context dependent and subject to historical and cultural variation. As Hood-Williams and Harrison say earlier in their article, Butler's deconstruction of the categories of sex, gender and woman presents 'a far more open arena which can allow for *specific* enquiries' which 'is a welcome opening of fixed positions and of taken for granted assumptions within the field' (1998: 89). It is precisely these specific enquiries that Butler's account of performativity shows need to be undertaken to demonstrate how this works in each of these registers and in differing social and cultural contexts.

Indeed, Butler herself does this at times in relation to the process of racialization as well as sex/gender (some of which is discussed in Chapter 3). However, that Butler herself does not identify all of the possible registers in her account of gender performativity does not in itself impugn the theoretical strength of her account. How could she possibly be expected to? It is rather that her account of performativity provides the philosophical framework and methodological tools for such enquiries.

Plus, it must be remembered that although patriarchy as a universal concept and a universal system may well have been displaced in sociological enquiry, as Hood-Williams and Harrison suggest (having fallen from grace along with other grand narratives), feminist accounts of the workings of gender relations, sex and sexuality continue to point to the hierarchies and asymmetry involved, and continue to find more and more sophisticated ways of showing that patriarchal social relations continue to structure the lives, bodies, experiences and even psyches of women and the possibilities open to them.

Conclusion

Ironically, Butler brings a theatrical notion of acts to the context of phenomenological accounts of constituting acts, in the production of gendered subjectivity, in order to avoid the 'individualist assumptions' that underlie such accounts. The aim was to set individual acts in a wider social context and the main thrust of this was to uncover the power relations that systematically produce gender-based inequalities, the oppression of women and heterosexual hegemony. Yet her account is often presumed to be presenting an individualist and voluntarist theatrical model itself, and is accused of ignoring these structural features (including the material basis of women's oppression) and the social context of individual action. The trouble is that when she says that identity is the product of social and political regulation rather than an innate property of individuals, the social and political regulation to which she refers is manifested in signifying practices, so it is signifying practices (as the source of the constitution of meaning) that is the focus of her work. Many feminists take this to be a different level of analysis to concrete political reality.

Much of Butler's work after *Gender Trouble* involves developing her account of performativity in ways that demonstrate that this is not the case. It is rather an attempt to accommodate the structural features and social context of individual action in a way that retains the possibility of resistance and change whilst continuing to recognize the limitations of the humanist view of the subject as the source of agency. Most significantly, this critique of gender categories does not gesture towards some sort of post-gender position as if it were possible to simply 'step outside' of gender categories, as is sometimes thought to be the case. It rather involves demonstrating the simultaneous necessity and contingency of identity categories. This is nowhere clearer than in her account of the materialization of the body, which is the topic of the next chapter.

2 Body matters: from construction to materialization

It is often argued that Butler's account of performativity neglects the materiality of the specifically female body. Theorizing gender as performative in *Gender Trouble* involved denaturalizing the body and rejecting the idea that bodies in some way cause gender. Butler aimed to show that bodily categories such as sex, gender and sexuality are products of discourses and power relations rather than natural effects of the body, as discussed in Chapter 1. She argued instead that it is through the various bodily categories that 'a sexed nature or "a natural sex" is produced and established as "prediscursive", prior to culture, a politically neutral surface on which culture acts' (1990a: 7). Understanding the body as the foundation of these bodily categories is a product of regimes of power/knowledge in a Foucauldian sense, which have vested interests 'in keeping the body bounded and constituted by the markers of sex' (p. 129).

Hence, rather than accepting the materiality of the body as something that is simply given in biology or nature, Butler develops a view of the body following Nietzsche and Foucault as a construction, a product of the effects of power. She also adapts insights from a range of theorists, including in particular de Beauvoir, Kristeva and Wittig, to argue that gender norms play a prominent role in the process of that construction. Although she rejects Kristeva's view of the maternal body, because such a position reifies the very categories that she wants to argue are a product of compulsory heterosexuality and phallogocentrism, she draws on her work in *Powers of Horror* to rethink the 'boundary and surface of bodies as politically constructed' (p. xii). She builds on Monique Wittig's view that 'morphology itself is a consequence of a hegemonic conceptual scheme' (p. xii) and that the category of sex is a political category (as discussed in Chapter 1). From Simone de Beauvoir she takes the idea that 'one is not born a woman but becomes one'.

In *The Second Sex*, de Beauvoir is concerned with the way that women are construed as some kind of deviation, some kind of embodied, particular 'other' to a disembodied, universal, male subject, and how this construction of women could be overcome. Indeed, much of *The Second Sex* involves an attempt to reveal the implications of the misogynistic bias in intellectual life that produced such a view of women's 'nature'. De Beauvoir wanted to challenge arguments that women are inherently inferior to men due to their biological make-up. She therefore aimed to find a way for women to transcend their biology, and thus their position of 'otherness', so that they too could become subjects, with freedom, in the same way as men. Consequently, she emphasized the social nature of identity and argued emphatically that any apparent 'nature' of women is culturally based rather than biologically given. In order to do this, she drew on the phenomenology of Maurice Merleau-Ponty to develop a view of the body as a 'situation', endowed with cultural meaning, and suggested that becoming a woman involves a kind of cultural compulsion.

Butler incorporates de Beauvoir's suggestion that becoming a woman involves a cultural compulsion into her own account of the performativity of gender, which involves 'enforced cultural performances'. However, although she notes with approval the phenomenological idea of the body as a situation endowed with cultural meaning, Butler rejects the binary thinking in relation to the mind/body dualism involved in de Beauvoir's account. Butler argues that whilst de Beauvoir aims to avoid the mind/body split, she ultimately fails to do so, as her account is based on a theory of embodiment that is 'limited by the uncritical reproduction of the Cartesian distinction between freedom and the body' (1990a: 12). Butler argues that this distinction ultimately accepts, and reinvokes, the gender hierarchy implicit in the mind/body distinction, in which the mind is associated with maleness, freedom and transcendence, and the body with femininity, bondage and subjugation.[1]

Furthermore, Butler rejects what she sees as the humanism

involved in de Beauvoir's account: the view of the body as something separate to that which animates it, and from the subject
who, as Butler sees it, comes into being through the process of
its materialization, but is not separable from that process. Hence
Butler rejects the idea implicit within de Beauvoir's account that
there is 'an agent, a cogito, who somehow takes on or appro-
priates that gender, and could in principle, take on some other
gender' (p. 8). Since, for Butler, the subject and the repetition of
acts are not separable in this way (as discussed in Chapter 1),
she sets the aspects of de Beauvoir's work that she adapts in the
context of a poststructuralist account of subjectivity that does
not involve such a view. In particular, Butler draws on Foucault's
account of subjectivity in which the body itself, as well as sex
and sexuality, is conceived as a construction, a discursive effect
of power and normalization. As discussed in Chapter 1, Butler
develops the notion of performativity to explain how this works
in relation to gender identity, aspects that Foucault did not
really consider.

To reiterate then, Butler's approach involves analysing the
performative production of sexed identity, concentrating in
Gender Trouble on the processes through which sex and gender
come to be conceived as natural extensions of a biological body,
rather than taking the materiality (or biology) of the body as a
starting point. She argues that it is not so much that the body is
the material or 'sexually factic' ground on which gender operates, as is implied in the sex/gender distinction; it is more that
the body is performatively produced as such through the sedimentation of 'corporeal styles' in a 'stylized repetition of acts'.
The 'real' and the 'sexually factic' are conceived as 'phantasmatic constructions – illusions of substance – that bodies are
compelled to approximate, but never can' (p. 146) in these
social performances.

This account was then criticized for neglecting the materiality
of the body. Perhaps not surprisingly, however, since materiality
is not something that is immediately given or graspable in
Butler's view, the move from construction to materialization
that is her response to this criticism, in *Bodies that Matter*,
involves a critique of the concept of materiality itself. It also
involves rethinking the meaning of construction beyond that
implied in the dichotomy of materiality (or essentialism) and

construction. Her aim is to highlight the difficulties in posing the materiality of the body as the ground of feminist enquiry. Instead she wants to show that 'to invoke matter is to invoke a sedimented history of sexual hierarchy and sexual erasures which should surely be the object of feminist inquiry' (1993a: 49), rather than the starting point.

Matter is thus reconceived, 'not as a site or surface, but as *a process of materialization that stabilizes over time to produce the effect of boundary, fixity and surface we call matter*'. Furthermore, she goes on: 'That matter is always materialized has, I think, to be thought in relation to the productive and, indeed, materializing effects of regulatory power in a Foucauldian sense' (pp. 9–10, original emphasis). Hence, the 'matter' or materiality of bodies becomes an effect of power and signification, 'such that the matter of bodies will be indissociable from the regulatory norms that govern their materialization and the signification of those material effects' (p. 2). In other words, her concern with materiality in *Bodies that Matter* is a concern with the ways in which the regulatory norms of 'sex' performatively constitute the materiality of the body. Moreover, the category of 'sex', which she now says she neglected in *Gender Trouble*, becomes a cultural norm that governs the materialization of the body.

In order to show how this regulatory power works in the production or materialization of sexed bodies, Butler further develops her account of performativity along speech act lines. She turns to the notions of iteration and citation in Derrida's reworking of Austin's speech act theory and reformulates the performativity of gender as a matter of the citation of the norms of sex, as discussed in the previous chapter. The sustained social performances that amounted 'to a stylized repetition of acts' in *Gender Trouble* become a matter of 'the forcible and reiterative practice of regulatory sexual regimes' (Butler 1993a: 15) in *Bodies that Matter*. Reiterative practice becomes a matter of citationality, rather than performance, and citationality becomes a matter of the body's materialization. The earlier attention to gender as corporeal styles is thus replaced by a concern with the body's materialization as sexed, through a process involving the citation and re-citation of norms.

Furthermore, this reformulation of materiality and performativity also involves a turn to the psychoanalytic categories of identification and melancholia. In 'The Lesbian Phallus and the Morphological Imaginary' and 'Phantasmatic Identification and the Assumption of Sex' (both in 1993a) Butler draws on the work of Freud and Lacan to argue that identificatory processes are crucial to the forming of sexed materiality but at the same time argues that the social norms that regulate identificatory projections can be construed as heterosexual imperatives. She is thus able to argue that 'the regime of heterosexuality operates to circumscribe and contour the "materiality" of sex, and that "materiality" is formed and sustained through and as a materialization of regulatory norms that are in part those of heterosexual hegemony' (Butler 1993a: 15) and to focus on the role of the heterosexist imperative in enabling certain sexed identifications and excluding others. This move allows her to focus on the way that the category of sex, and thus sexual difference, is not immutable, as it often seems to be taken to be in feminist theories that focus on sexual difference rather than gender (e.g. Kristeva, Irigaray). In this formulation it rather becomes a normative constraint through which bodies come into being in the process of their materialization.

Butler's rethinking of the materiality of the body, then, continues to highlight the 'instability produced by the effort to fix the site of the sexed body' (p. 16), which was an important aspect of *Gender Trouble*, though the manner in which she does this and the areas on which she focuses have shifted considerably. One significant change is that the earlier focus on the role of gender in the production of sex has been replaced by a consideration of how the category of sex is itself produced as a regulatory norm; and a consideration of the role of this regulatory norm in the materialization of the body and, at the same time, the production of sexed subjects. Furthermore, the focus is now on the way in which the instability involved in the production of the sexed body 'challenges the boundaries of discursive intelligibility' (p. 16) in the various contexts that are considered.[2]

Butler conceives of a realm of abject unintelligible bodies which 'don't matter' but which form a necessary constitutive outside to the realm of intelligible bodies that 'do matter'. However, this realm is not conceived as a reverse discourse in a Foucauldian sense but as an excluded realm which therefore represents the possibility of return as in a psychoanalytic model. Although she still wants to retain a notion of gender practices as sites of 'critical agency' (that is resistance, transformation and change), the subversive possibilities of parody and drag that were highlighted in *Gender Trouble* are replaced in *Bodies that Matter* by a concern with the less theatrical notions of citationality and iteration. It is these that allow the possibility of agency and change. Although greater attention is also given to the question of 'race' and racialization as intrinsic to the performative production of sexed and gendered bodies, and as subversive of 'the monolithic workings of the heterosexual imperative' (p. 18), the main focus in *Bodies that Matter* is on 'sex', gender and sexuality – or as she puts it in the sub-title, 'on the discursive limits of "sex" '.[3] As Butler says in the introduction:

> The point here is not only to remark upon the difficulty of delivering through discourse the uncontested site of sex. Rather, the point is to show that the uncontested status of 'sex' within the heterosexual dyad secures the workings of certain symbolic orders, and that its contestation calls into question where and how the limits of symbolic intelligibility are set.
>
> (p. 16)

The main concern thus continues to be with a critique of the workings of the heterosexual imperative, or 'heterosexual hegemony' as she now puts it, 'in the crafting of matters sexual and political' and how to challenge that (p. xii). This continues to involve a critique of the 'prevailing truth regime of "sex" ', that she takes 'to be pervasively heterosexist' (p. 233). But it also involves a concern with the significance of 'queer' for 'collective contestations' (p. 228) that has shifted from a focus on the possibilities of parody and drag that were considered in *Gender Trouble*, to include a focus on how ' "queerness" might be understood not only as an example of citational politics, but as a reworking of abjection into political agency that might explain why "citationality" has contemporary political promise' (p. 21). Plus, there is a consideration of the possibilities of a redescription of the symbolic (though this is not to be confused with

Irigaray's strategy of establishing an alternative female imaginary, as will become clear later).

In sum then, Butler's critique of the concept of materiality and move from construction to materialization in *Bodies that Matter* involves four main aspects that are examined in this chapter. These are:

- rethinking constructivism beyond the materiality/construction dichotomy and theorizing materiality as a matter of materialization;
- rethinking the category of 'sex' as a cultural norm through which bodies are materialized;
- developing the notion of performativity through Derrida's critique of speech act theory and the notions of iterability and citationality involved in that; and
- thinking performativity through psychoanalysis, especially the notions of identification and morphogenesis.

Matter becomes a question of materialization; the materialization of the body becomes a question of the performativity of gender; the performativity of gender becomes a matter of the citation of the regulatory norms of sex. It is through these regulatory norms that the body is materialized as sexed and gendered, though these are articulated with other regulatory norms which materialize the body as 'raced', classed, aged, etc. The possibility for resistance comes from the repetition involved in iterability and citationality.

Furthermore, these moves develop the temporal aspect in her account of performativity, an aspect which Butler claims is absent in Foucault's account (as discussed in Chapter 1).[4] They also allow her to speak of the 'constitutive instabilities' at the heart of this process. This is important because it is precisely because sex becomes naturalized as a sedimented effect of the reiterations of norms that enables the possibility of change through the 'gaps and fissures' that open up. These are produced by that which escapes being fixed by the norm, the excess, in a Derridean sense: 'This instability is the *de*constituting possibility in the very process of repetition, the power that undoes the very effects by which "sex" is stabilized, the possibility to put the consolidation of the norms of "sex" into a potentially productive crisis' (p. 10). However, whilst it is the possibility of such a potentially productive crisis that forms the basis of her 'strategy' and hope for change, this is also what critics claim is politically debilitating for feminist projects.

From construction to materialization

Butler thus argues that thinking the materiality of the body involves rethinking the meaning of construction beyond that implied in the dichotomies of essentialism and/or materialism versus construction. It is just such a dichotomy that sustains the sex/gender distinction in which sex is conceived as the material base upon which the edifice of gender is built in a process of social construction. She argues instead that this view of sex as the material base to the social construction of gender is itself a cultural construct – a product of phallogocentrism and compulsory heterosexuality – that serves to naturalize the body and the categories of sex and gender. Indeed, Butler is careful to distinguish her account of construction from others in the introduction to *Bodies that Matter*, and to explain her move from 'construction to materialization'.

The main difference between Butler's account and others is that she refuses to distinguish between something essential in one way or another (e.g. biology, materiality, matter or the psyche), upon which an act of construction works, and any acts of social construction themselves. She combines a kind of Nietzschean genealogy in which the body is interpretation all the way down, with the Derridean insight that there is always excess to representation and interpretation (this is important for her view of change and transformation and will be discussed in more detail later). From this perspective it makes no sense to accept a materiality/construction distinction because there is simply no way we can get outside of our cultural frameworks or, to be more precise, outside of language and signification in order to get at that something essential, including, in this case, the matter or materiality of the body.

Butler thus questions the acceptance of the materiality of sex as given that underpins much feminist thinking, including feminist epistemologies, feminist ethics and various analyses of gender. At the same time, however, she insists that her move from construction to materialization involves neither a negation of materiality, nor the suggestion that bodies are immaterial. It is rather an attempt to stress the materiality of significations and the regulatory frameworks through which bodies come into being and embodied subjects achieve cultural intelligibility (or not). Rather than starting with the apparent facticity of the materiality of the body or sex, in a typically deconstructive move, she asks instead 'how and why "materiality" has become a sign of irreducibility, that is, how is it that the materiality of sex is understood as that which only *bears* cultural constructions and therefore cannot be a construction?' (Butler 1993a: 28, original emphasis). She argues that this questioning helps to reveal the matrix of power that produces the view of materiality – in this case the materiality of 'sex', the body, and sexual difference – as something that stands outside of the process of construction.

Butler thus advocates pursuing a critical genealogy of the concept of materiality. In *Bodies that Matter* this involves a genealogy of the concept of materiality in the history of philosophy in which the main focus is Irigaray's deconstruction of the form/matter distinction in Plato, and her claim that materiality is constituted through an exclusion and denigration of the feminine. Butler argues that the main point of this exercise, which focused 'more on the sex of materiality than the matter of sex' was to show that:

> We may seek to return to matter as prior to discourse to ground our claims about sexual difference only to discover that matter is fully sedimented with discourses on sex and sexuality that prefigure and constrain the uses to which that term can be put.
>
> (p. 29)

Her concern is thus with the political significance of the production and regulation of the matter of bodies. She is concerned to deconstruct the notions of the body and materiality, in order 'to displace them from the contexts in which they have been deployed as instruments of oppressive power' (p. 17). So to pose the question in terms of discourse, or construction, versus materiality, as her critics do, misses the critical point. Her

critical/political point is that deconstructing the materiality of
bodies 'provides the conditions to mobilize the signifier in the
service of an alternative production' (p. 17). It reveals the category of sex to be a principle of production and regulation
rather than simply a representation of a prior materiality.

Butler develops this point in 'Contingent Foundations: Feminism and the Question of Postmodernism' (Butler 1992a). Citing Wittig and Foucault, who both view the category of sex as
something that 'produces and regulates the intelligibility of the
materiality of the body' (p. 17) in the service of reproductive
sexuality as a compulsory order, Butler argues that the production of sex is itself a material violence. Hence, deconstructing
the category of sex and the matter of bodies in this way is not to
'question the urgency or credibility of sex or violence as political
issues, but rather show that the way their very materiality is
circumscribed is fully political' (p. 19). This becomes clearer
when examining what does and does not count as evidence of
violence and rape as far as the legal system and certain courts in
the USA are concerned, and the difficulties involved in establishing that a rape has occurred. Butler argues that there is already
violence at work in these arenas, foreclosing the possibilities of
what will and will not count, and involving the category of sex
as a principle of production. She refers to the trial of a gang rape
in New Bedford in which the plaintiff is asked: 'If you're living
with a man, what are you doing running around the streets
getting raped?' (p. 18). Butler demonstrates how this questioning involves the idea that it is the woman's sex, in its materiality,
that somehow causes the rape, and that she colludes in it by
stepping outside the domestic realm (which is where she belongs
as the partner of a man). The woman is raped because of her sex
but also because of her sex the woman herself is blamed for
putting herself in a situation where this could occur. It is difficult
for her to establish that a rape has occurred, not only because
some states require twelve separate pieces of evidence, but
because there is a presumption that she must have wanted it
or she wouldn't have been there. The category of sex can then
be seen as a principle of 'production, intelligibility and regulation' rather than merely one of representation 'which enforces
a violence and rationalizes it after the fact' (p. 19). Violence,
from a poststructuralist prospective is not only the physical (and

psychological) violence involved in the rape, which it is so difficult to prove, but the violence involved in the production of meaning and intelligibility, which allows some meanings to prevail and forecloses others. Therefore, Butler advocates putting the categories of 'sex' and 'violence' into quotation marks, in order to denaturalize them and indicate that they are sites of political debate to 'show that the way their very materiality is circumscribed is fully political' (p. 19).[5]

This is a move that is reminiscent of Heidegger's strategy of putting the concept of Being '*sous rature*' (under erasure). Heidegger developed this strategy because the concept of Being is a metaphysical concept. This means that its meaning cannot be decided because it is simply inexplicable in any other than metaphysical terms. Heidegger's strategy involved crossing out the word Being but then letting it stand while crossed out in recognition of the need to continue to use it, despite its undecidability. Butler's use of quotation marks around the concepts of sex and violence can be seen as a similar strategy.

Although Butler is not concerned with metaphysical questions concerning the nature of sex, gender and the body *per se*, her critique of these categories involves addressing the metaphysical presuppositions that inform dominant understandings of them. These are based on Cartesian understandings of human being and the metaphysics of substance and presence that, from her poststructuralist perspective, she finds untenable and that she aims to avoid in her account of performativity (see also Chapter 1). However, she does not suggest abandoning such categories altogether but rather aims to reveal the instability on which they are based, the violence and exclusions that underpin any apparent coherence. Furthermore, Derrida's critique of the indeterminacy of the category of 'woman' and 'meaning' in *Spurs* (Derrida 1979) would shed light on Butler's critique of sexual difference as something that is not determinable in ontological terms. It is rather produced as an immutable, ontological category within the framework of the heterosexual (and heterosexist) imaginary, which governs the materialization of bodies and the formation of sexed identities.

Butler insists that this is not a matter of the negation of the body or of the concept of matter as: 'To call a presupposition into question is not the same as doing away with it' (Butler

1993a: 30). It is rather that a deconstructive move such as this frees the body and the concept of matter from metaphysical constraints and opens them up to political scrutiny. Although this may problematize epistemological accounts of the body, it also offers the possibility of alternative understandings of bodies, in their materiality, and the possibility of this is of major concern to Butler.

Is materiality a linguistic product?

Butler's argument is, therefore, not that the materiality of bodies is nothing but a linguistic product, but rather that the concept of materiality is inescapably bound up with signification. Although this is a very complex argument, basically it involves applying a poststructuralist understanding of the separation of the signifier (the word or image) from the signified (the concept), and of both of these from the referent (the thing in the world), to the matter of the body as putative referent. Butler's basic premise seems to be that the difference between matter and signification is one of radical incommensurability, although not in the sense of two discrete entities. Again, this is a complex matter and the precise relationship is not always fully articulated in Butler's work. In her account, neither matter nor signification can be completely separated from the other, nor can either fully exceed the other, or be reduced to the other. Although 'they remain radically different', there can be no access to a pure materiality outside of, or before, signification. Importantly though, Butler does not take this to imply a repudiation or negation of matter so much as a demand for an examination of the exclusions involved in the process of materialization, and an examination of the materiality of the signifier in that process. Her point is that 'every effort to refer to materiality takes place through a signifying process which, in its phenomenality, is always already material' (Butler 1993a: 68). Hence, 'there can be no reference to a pure materiality except via materiality' (p. 68).

Nevertheless, Butler also says that: 'The radical difference between referent and signified is the site where the materiality of language and that of the world which it seeks to signify are perpetually negotiated' (p. 69). This could seem to imply that, despite her insistence to the contrary, Butler still retains a

matter/form distinction. Furthermore, speaking of a 'radical difference' would certainly seem to involve a distinction between
language, or signification, and matter, as would the suggestion
that they are 'radically incommensurable'. Yet at the same time,
Butler insists that matter cannot be said to exist apart from language. Not only is this apparently contradictory, it leaves no
room for a distinction between language and materiality even in
analytical terms, as Hull (1997: 26) argues. In which case, could
it be that Butler has gone too far in her attempt to focus on the
materiality of language and signification, and capitulated to the
vagaries of idealism? This is the view of some critics. Kirby, for
example, suggests that this is the case. She questions Butler's
refutation of the charge of linguisticism and argues instead:

> If we are only ever dealing with the signification of matter
> rather than the stuff of matter as such, then constructedness
> cannot be opposed to the fact of matter: the mutually consti-
> tutive implications of their embrace now appears within the
> realm of ideality.
>
> (Kirby 1997: 107)

However, this type of either/or scenario involves just the kind of
metaphysical opposition that Butler's account of performativity
aims to avoid. Thus in her view, the suggestion that her account
of the relationship between matter and signification amounts to
a form of idealism is based on the assumption of a metaphysical
opposition between materialism and idealism, which is undermined in a poststructuralist perspective. Indeed, her account of
the performativity of discourse in the materialization of sex is an
attempt to further demonstrate the limitations of this distinction
by focusing on the significance of language and signification
without reducing everything to them. Thus, she insists that the
view of materiality involved in her account challenges traditional and common-sense understandings of reference, but it
does not involve some form of idealism, or nominalism – the
reduction of 'reality' to a matter of words. Hence she argues:

> To claim that discourse is formative is not to claim that
> it originates, causes or exhaustively composes that which it
> concedes; rather, it is to claim that there is no reference to a

pure body which is not at the same time further *formation* of that body. In this sense the linguistic capacity to refer to sexed bodies is not denied, but the very meaning of 'referentiality' is altered. In philosophical terms the constative is always to some degree performative.

(Butler 1993a: 10–11, original emphasis)

This is a complex philosophical point, however, and one reason that the view of materiality it involves is problematic is that it is counter-intuitive in everyday terms. This is because it involves a rejection of the common-sense understanding of materiality as a reality, or referent, outside language that is simply and directly referred to in language. It seems irrefutably obvious that there is a reality outside language and representation, a difference between 'words' and 'things', and that the physicality of the body in its impermanence and susceptibility to pain and disease bears testimony to that. Butler's point on this matter, however, is that this irrefutability in no way provides a way of knowing these experiences in an essential way without the mediation of cultural frameworks, language and signification. 'To posit by way of language a materiality outside of language is still to posit that materiality, and the materiality so posited will retain that positing as its constitutive condition' (p. 30).

Although this sounds a little like a Hegelian postulation, it might be better to consider it in terms of Derrida's critique of Austin and generalization of the performative in 'Signature, Event, Context' (Derrida 1988). This was discussed in the previous chapter in relation to the notions of iterability and citationality, and Butler's attempt to develop her account of performativity in less theatrical and voluntaristic terms than sometimes seemed to be the case in *Gender Trouble*. However, her account of matter and materiality is also indebted to other aspects of Derrida's work that are involved in this critique, in particular *différance*, his reformulation of the concept of 'writing', and his critique of 'logocentrism', all of which are related to his critique of the 'metaphysics of presence' (which was also discussed in Chapter 1).[6]

Derrida, speech acts and performativity

In his speech act theory, Austin distinguishes between speech acts that are a matter of communication, and performative speech acts which actually bring into being that which they name, e.g. the marriage ceremony in which a couple are pronounced 'husband and wife', the naming of a ship, the pronouncement of 'guilty' by a judge in a law court. He thus distinguishes between *constative* speech, which is descriptive only and *performative* speech, which is productive. In order to make this distinction, Austin differentiates between serious speech acts which will be performative, and non-serious speech acts (such as acting, playing, unauthorized citing) which will not be performative by drawing up a list of exclusions. These are based on the context and the intentions of the speaker. It is the context and intentions of the speech that fixes the meaning of speech acts and renders them authoritative and therefore performative (or not). However, Derrida brings his critique of 'presence' and his deconstruction of the literal/metaphorical distinction to bear on this and demonstrates that the question of context cannot be fixed in the way presumed by Austin. The non-serious speech acts that are excluded as exceptions to the rule, and thus as contingent possibilities, are in fact the model for performative utterance in general.

In order to see this, it's necessary to move from the idea of writing in a traditional sense (which Austin excludes in his speech act theory) to Derrida's reformulation of 'writing' in *Of Grammatology* (1974) to include spoken as well as written marks. Derrida demonstrates that the speech/writing opposition, in which speech is privileged as more immediate than writing, is based on the suppression of the role of 'writing' in the production and interpretation of speech. He demonstrates that speech is also a form of 'writing'. It is no more immediate or self-present than writing because it too is made up of a series of marks whose intelligibility stems from their relation to other marks in a general economy of meaning. This whole process is sometimes described as a kind of 'graphematic structure'. It is this graphematic structure that provides the possibility for interpretation, experience, meaning, and subjectivity, even as it simultaneously marks the impossibility of full presence in any of these arenas. They are all constituted within a never-ending process of referral and deferral, differing and differentiation. It is simply not possible to get outside of this graphematic process; to get outside of *différance*. In demonstrating this, Derrida establishes that there is no meaning outside of interpretation, outside of this graphematic structure (only excess, which is that which is not captured in interpretation). Importantly, this undermines the possibility of privileged access to self-present meanings and (the fixing of) intentions, on which Austin's account of the successful functioning of performative speech relies.

Derrida's point is that if we accept the graphematic structure of all locution, of *différance*, then we can see that speech, as well as writing, is marked by the absence of presence and the possibility of iteration. In this case, not only is the impossibility of the fixing of meaning and/or context highlighted, but also, the possibility of failure becomes a structural element (along with the possibility of the absence of a speaker and a receiver). Moreover all utterances become performative. Hence the ritual that Austin cites as the binding context (e.g. the marriage ceremony, the launch of a ship) is replaced by Derrida with the notion of iterability: 'Ritual is not an eventuality, but, as iterability, is a structural characteristic of every mark' (Derrida 1982: 324). As Butler puts it in another context (in a discussion of Bourdieu), Derrida 'substitutes the term "iterability" for ritual, thus establishing a structural account of repetition in the place of a more semantically compounded sense of social ritual' (Butler 1997a: 165–6, n. 3). Importantly, moreover, for Butler:

> The binding power that Austin attributes to the speaker's intention in such illocutionary acts is more properly attributable to a citational force of the speaking, the iterability that establishes the authority of the speech act, but which establishes the non-circular character of that act. In this sense, every 'act' is an echo or citational chain, and it is its citationality that constitutes its performative force.
>
> (Butler 1993a: 282, n. 5)

What is at stake here is the replacement of the logic of repetition and non-contradiction, on which Western metaphysics is based, with the graphic of iterability. Hence, Derrida takes the premise that the possibility of communication rests on the condition that every mark, or sign, can be cited. But he adds to that the notion of iterability in order to tease out the implications of this citability, beyond those assumed in speech act theory. He employs the 'graphic of iterability' to develop the notion of citation away from a mere mechanical repetition, to suggest instead a repeatability which implies otherness and the possibility of alteration within it. Iterability is an iter-ation and, as such, in a typical deconstructive strategy, it undermines the possibility of self-identity or the fixing of meaning. Hence, precisely because any mark can be cited, it can 'break with every given context, and engender infinitely new contexts in an absolutely nonsaturable fashion' (Derrida 1982: 320). Moreover, Derrida continues: 'This does not suppose that the mark is valid outside its context, but on the contrary that there are only contexts without any center of absolute anchoring' (p. 320). Since the undecidability of context is the condition of possibility of any mark (whether written or spoken), the fixing of meaning becomes impossible. To think otherwise is to succumb to the myth of presence.

Unfortunately however, as Derrida himself insists, it is not possible simply to move beyond the metaphysical tradition in an act of volition; all that can be done is to deconstruct the founding elements of it. Hence:

> Deconstruction does not consist in passing from one concept to another, but in overturning and displacing a conceptual order, as well as a non-conceptual order with which the conceptual order is articulated. For example, writing as a classical concept carries with it predicates which have been subordinated, excluded or held in reserve by forces and according to necessities to be analyzed. It is these predicates (I have mentioned some) whose force of generality, generalization, and generativity find themselves liberated, grafted onto a 'new' concept of writing which also corresponds to whatever has resisted the former organization of forces, which has constituted the remainder irreducible to the dominant force which organized the – to say it quickly – logocentric hierarchy.
>
> (pp. 329–30)

One response to all this is to drown in the impossibility of presence: to dwell on the impossibility of language, the impossibility of saying anything in an essential sense. A more fruitful response would be to focus instead on the productive power of language in its performativity and its materiality; and on the positive possibilities opened up by the notions of excess and iterability. This is what Butler does. Indeed, it is because she wants to allow for resistance and change in her otherwise very Foucauldian account of gendered embodiment – and in so doing avoid what she terms 'Foucault's paradox' – that she draws on the notions of iterability, temporality and citationality in Derrida's reformulation of the performativity of language. This move allows her to retain the notion of sex/gender and bodies as discursive effects whilst avoiding the ultimate determinism that haunts Foucault's genealogy and notion of discourse, despite his aims to the contrary.

The trouble with Foucault's depiction of the body, the subject and social reality as discursive effects, products of power relations, is that it fails to show, theoretically, where the resistance comes from.[7] It also fails to fully theorize temporality, as Butler points out in a note to the introduction to *Bodies that Matter* (1993a: 245, n. 8), unlike Derrida's notion of iterability as discussed in Chapter 2. Iterability involves movement, temporization and spacing. It is not a mechanical repetition as would be implied in logocentric closure in which repetition is a repetition of the same. This is precisely because meaning is not fixed as deconstructive insights demonstrate. Such a mechanical repetition would depend on the suppression of difference and what Derrida terms *différance*. Furthermore, *différance* and iterability open up the space for concern with otherness or alterity, that which exceeds logocentric closure. This is an important point because it is this that allows the possibility of difference, of change and transformation which is of vital importance to Butler.

Furthermore, although these insights highlight the role of language in the constitution of reality, both Derrida and Butler emphasize that they do not involve either a denial of reality in its materiality, or an insistence that it is only a matter of words. They do, however, involve rethinking the reference/representation, materiality/ideality dichotomies and questioning the status of the material world as something that stands outside significatory frameworks and shapes them; which is precisely Butler's point in relation to the materiality of the body.[8] When considered in light of these insights, it becomes clear that the materiality of the body (including its biology, its physiology, its corporeal specificity) can only be understood through the mediation of interpretation in which the fixing of meaning is both temporary and retrospective. Therefore it follows that the materiality of its corporeality does not fix the meaning of the body, although logocentric representations may act as if this were the case. Indeed, the crux of the matter is that the meaning of bodies can never be permanently fixed or sealed. Butler's focus is thus on the performative production of sexed identity and the processes through which bodies are materialized as sexed, rather than taking the materiality (or biology) of the body as a starting point. One way in which she does this in *Bodies that Matter* is by thinking her account of performativity through aspects of psychoanalysis.

Psychoanalysis and the materialization of bodies

Butler draws on psychoanalytic insights to develop her account of the phantasmatic status of the body, her view that bodies only come to be through imaginary frameworks, to show *how* bodies are materialized as appropriately sexed. She argues that this occurs through identificatory processes involving the psychic incorporation of heterosexual norms. However, she also wants to reveal the limits to these psychoanalytic insights, in particular the reification of normative heterosexuality and the duality of sexual difference which, she argues, is foundational to the work of both Freud and Lacan.[9]

One of the ways that she is able to do this in *Bodies that Matter* is by rethinking the Lacanian view of the symbolic through a Derridean notion of performativity. Rather than a quasi-permanent structure, as Lacan's account would seem to suggest, from this perspective the symbolic becomes the 'temporalized regulation of signification' and, as such, part of the regulatory schema through which bodies are materialized as sexed.

Hence, in the 'Lesbian Phallus and the Morphological Imaginary' and in 'Phantasmatic Identification and the Assumption of Sex' (both in Butler 1993a), she turns to the work of Freud and Lacan to argue that identificatory processes are crucial to the forming of sexed materiality. In the former she takes Freud's claim, in *The Ego and the Id*, that 'The ego is first and foremost a bodily ego: it is not merely a surface entity, but is itself the projection of a surface' (cited in Butler 1993a: 59) to suggest that the body is an imaginary formation that comes into being through the 'somaticizing' activity of the psyche. Furthermore she argues that Freud's essay 'On Narcissus: An Introduction', on the relationship between pain and consciousness and the erotogenicity of body parts, when read in conjunction with *The Ego and the Id*, implies that the psyche and the physical body are indissoluble. Drawing on Freud's suggestion in his analysis of the erotogenicity of body parts, that a body part requires 'phantasmatic partitioning to bring it into psychic experience', Butler suggests that:

> If erotogenicity is produced through the conveying of a bodily activity through an idea, then the idea and the conveying are phenomenologically coincident. As a result, it would not be possible to speak about a body part that precedes and gives rise to an idea, for it is the idea that emerges simultaneously with the phenomenologically accessible body, indeed that guarantees its accessibility.
>
> (Butler 1993a: 59)

She argues that this indicates that it is not that anatomy is a stable referent that is signified in an imaginary schema but that 'the very accessibility of anatomy is dependent on this schema and coincident with it' (p. 65). Indeed, any description of the body, including those in scientific discourse, 'takes place through the circulation and validation of such an imaginary schema' (p. 66). The point is that the psyche is not a grid through which a pre-given body appears. It is rather that 'the very contours of the body are the sites that vacillate between the psychic and the material' (p. 66). Hence, 'bodily contours and morphology are not merely implicated in an irreducible tension between the psychic and the material but *are* that tension' (p. 66, original emphasis).

Butler is making these rather complex distinctions in order to counter a charge of idealism. She does not want to suggest that it is the *idea* that produces the *thing* (i.e. the body) in any kind of reductionist way but rather seeks to demonstrate that the two go hand in hand in a sort of Kantian way. The psyche could be understood as 'the mode by which the body is given; the condition and contour of the givenness' (p. 66). What motivates it, however, is not the materiality of the body but rather a 'demand in and for language', a 'that without which' no psychic operation can proceed. This is 'a constitutive demand that mobilizes psychic action from the start' (p. 67).

It might be useful to explain this reference to Kant for those who do not have a philosophical background. Kant distinguishes between the 'thing in itself', the '*noumenon*' which cannot be known, and the world of objects as it is known to us – the phenomenological world which is given form through the 'categenological imperative'. The categories involved in this, however, are given in the structure of the mind and, for Kant precisely because of this, the form of the world that they give to us must be true. For Butler, however, the categories through which we give shape to the world are not given in the structure of the mind but are products of language and signification. Hence, from her 'queer', poststructuralist perspective, she argues that the view of the body as an imaginary formation needs to be considered in the context of a 'theory of signification as an effect and token of sexual difference' (p. 66).

In order to do this she draws on Lacan, who develops Freud's view of the body as an imaginary formation in this way. For Lacan the body, or morphology, 'can be sustained in its phantasmatic integrity only through submitting to langauge and the mark of sexual difference' (p. 72) in the process of identification (and morphogenesis) marked by the mirror stage. This involves being named in the symbolic order that is structured by kinship relations which are shaped by the law of the father. It is this that constitutes the coherence of the body, not 'a natural boundary or organic telos' (p. 72). Butler suggests that if this is the case, then 'the name which installs gender and kinship works as a politically invested and investing performative' (p. 72). Hence, '[t]o be named is thus to be inculcated into that law and to be formed, bodily, in accordance with that law' (p. 72). The body (and that of others) thus becomes the product of a morphological scheme which is established through the mirror stage.

However, for Lacan this process involves a view of the symbolic order in which it is shaped by the phallus and described in patriarchal terms as instituting the law of the father. Butler wants to challenge this view. She provides what she describes as a 'selective reading' (p. 72) of Lacan in 'The Mirror Stage' and 'The Signification of the Phallus', read through remarks in his Seminar, to take issue with his view of the workings of the symbolic order. Hence, she rejects Lacan's view of the fixity of the paternal law that marks the symbolic order as masculine and she rejects his view of the phallus as the inevitable foundation of the symbolic order.

She is able to do this because the Derridean notion of performativity allows her to rethink the Lacanian symbolic as the 'temporalized regulation of signification'. This move allows her to combine Lacan's view of sex as a normative position in language with a Foucauldian understanding of normativity as a regulatory ideal; and to develop the view of sex as a cultural norm that regulates the materialization of bodies. The incorporation of morphology that Lacan identifies in the mirror stage as a product of entry into the symbolic order and the accomplishment of sexed subjectivity becomes part of the regulatory schema through which bodies are materialized as sexed. Crucially for her view of change and transformation, she is thus able to argue that these regulatory schema are historically revisable, including the 'morphological imaginary' through which bodies come to be in the Lacanian symbolic order; rather than fixed and immutable as Lacan's account of the mirror stage would seem to suggest. Despite the contemporary privileging of the phallus it is, nevertheless, always in a process of signification and resignification. As such, the phallus is not so much the founding moment of the symbolic order, as Lacan would have it, but rather part of a reiterable signifying practice.

This then opens up the possibility for change, for resignification. Her argument in 'The Lesbian Phallus and the Morphological Imaginary' involves a consideration of the possibility of a 'lesbian phallus' and a discussion of the way in which the hegemonic imaginary 'constitutes itself through the naturalization of an exclusionary heterosexual morphology' (p. 91) to show *that this is not necessary*. Butler argues that, despite Lacan's protestations to the contrary in the 'Signification of the Phallus', the phallus is an imaginary effect (not a cause), therefore it cannot be that which secures the imaginary. It is an idealization that has no necessary relation to a masculine morphology and therefore could be called into question by 'an aggressive re-territorialization' (Butler 1993a: 86). Butler's aim is to rewrite the morphological imaginary in order to displace the symbolic of heterosexist sexual difference. This involves an attempt to expose the ways in which an exclusionary heterosexual morphology is naturalized, as she argues that it is through this that the phallus is understood in terms of masculine morphology: *That there is no necessary relation between the phallus and masculine body parts allows the possibility of a lesbian phallus*. Crucially, however, Butler's strategy is not to develop an alternative lesbian imaginary. Her aim is rather the more deconstructive move of disrupting and displacing the hegemonic heterosexual imaginary, which is shaped by a masculine signifying economy in which there is an imaginary association between the phallus and masculine body parts. Hence she says her strategy 'will be to show that the phallus can attach to a variety of organs, and that the efficacious disjoining of phallus from penis constitutes both a narcissistic wound to phallomorphism and the production of an anti-heterosexist sexual imaginary' (p. 262).

This rather long quote from 'The Lesbian Phallus' captures her project:

> The notion of the bodily ego in Freud and that of the projective idealization of the body in Lacan suggest that the very contours of the body, the delimitation of anatomy, are in part the consequence of an externalized identification. That identificatory process is itself motivated by a transfigurative wish. And that wishfulness proper to all morphogenesis is itself prepared and structured by a culturally complex signifying chain that not only constitutes sexuality, but establishes sexuality as a site where bodies and anatomies are perpetually reconstituted. If these central identifications cannot be strictly regulated, then the domain of the imaginary in which the body is partially constituted is marked by a constitutive vacillation. The anatomy is only 'given' through

its signification, and yet it appears to exceed that signification, to provide the elusive referent in relation to which the
variability of signification performs. Always already caught
up in the signifying chain by which sexual difference is negotiated, the anatomical is never outside its terms, and yet it is
also that which exceeds and compels that signifying chain,
that reiteration of difference, an insistent and inexhaustible
demand.

(p. 90)

Furthermore, the source of her optimism is this:

If the heterosexualization of identification and morphogenesis is historically contingent, however hegemonic, then
identifications, which are always already imaginary, as they
cross gender boundaries, reinstitute sexed bodies in variable
ways. In crossing these boundaries, such morphogenetic
identifications reconfigure the mapping of sexual difference
itself.

(p. 91)

Strategies for change

So Butler wants 'to reconfigure the mapping of sexual difference
itself'. Her reformulation of performativity through the insights
of psychoanalysis suggests that change needs to be directed at
the level of the imaginary (the morphological imaginary), since
it is through this that sexed identifications are produced and
bodies are materialized. However, this does not lead her to follow the kind of strategies suggested by sexual difference theorists, who are also concerned to rethink sexual difference and to
effect change at the level of the imaginary.[10] This is because their
view of the imaginary is conditioned by Lacan's view of the
symbolic as shaped by the phallus and instituting the law of
the father. It therefore necessarily devalues and/or excludes the
feminine, which is perceived in phallic terms only as a lack.
Indeed, from the perspective of sexual difference, it can be seen
that sexuality in psychoanalytic terms is *always* defined in terms
of masculine sexuality, which is why sexual difference theorists
tend to focus on reconstructive projects around the bodies of

women. Irigaray, for example, attempts to develop an alternative female imaginary in contention with the masculine one that governs the phallocentric signifying economy and, in so doing, develop an autonomous sexuality for women. Kristeva's approach is based on what she sees as the abjection of the maternal body from the masculine signifying economy (the symbolic order) and an attempt to recover a lost chora.

For Butler, however, such strategies are problematic in that they seem to accept the duality of sexual difference as in some sense given and irreducible (though not necessarily biologically, as some critics of Irigaray and Kristeva argue). This would be to succumb to the reification of sexual difference as it is constructed in normative heterosexuality. Butler is careful to avoid reifying sexual difference in this way. Hence, her focus is rather on the political effects of grounding the category of woman in the materiality of sex and posing the materiality of sex as causal. Her strategy for change involves denaturalizing and destabilizing the duality of sexual difference as it stands in the hegemonic symbolic order, which she characterizes as heterosexist, as well as phallocentric, in order to open up the possibilities for alternative imaginaries that are neither masculine nor feminine. Indeed, as she says in a footnote in which she distinguishes her strategy from Irigaray's: 'The implications of my strategy would seem to call into question the integrity of either a masculine or a feminine imaginary' (1993a: 262). It rather involves beginning 'to think the convergence and reciprocal formation of various imaginaries' and recognizing 'that sexual difference is neither more primary than other forms of social difference, nor is its formation understandable outside of a complex mapping of social power' (Butler 1995a: 142).

Moreover, as she makes clear in a discussion of this issue with Rosi Braidotti (Braidotti with Butler 1994), attempting to establish an autonomous sexuality for women cannot adequately accommodate lesbian desire, which may involve cross-identification with masculine norms. Indeed, for Butler it is precisely such cross-identification that reveals the instabilities in the hetero/homo binary in psychoanalytic accounts. She gives the examples of the 'phallicized dyke' and the 'feminized fag' (Butler 1993a: 110), as well as the lesbian femme and the masculine gay man. Focusing on the exclusion of the feminine and attempting to establish an autonomous sexuality for women does not address this instability. Nor, most importantly, does it challenge the separation of identity and desire that is foundational to psychoanalytic accounts of identity formation, whether based on Freud's Oedipalization of sexuality or Lacan's 'mirror stage'. Furthermore, it does not challenge the somewhat inadequate view of gay and lesbian desire as a matter of 'inversion' to which this separation gives rise. Indeed, in Lacan's account, the accession to the law of the father involves the repudiation and abjection of lesbian and gay forms of identification and desire. Hence, as Butler points out in 'Phantasmatic Identification and the Assumption of Desire' (in Butler 1993a), these sorts of complex crossings of desire and identification, which are not contained in and so contest the binary framework, are disallowed in the Lacanian symbolic. Indeed, their exclusion is crucial to the integrity of the binary framework in terms of sexual difference, normalized heterosexuality and abjected homosexuality, and in terms of 'feminized male homosexuality' and 'masculinized female homosexuality' (p. 104). Butler's strategy for change depends on bringing these abject subject positions into 'defiance and legitimacy' (p. 21). However, the aim is not to set them up as alternative viable subject positions but to contest and disrupt the hegemonic *heterosexist imaginary* that depends on their abjection and sustains a binary notion of sexual difference. This is a crucial distinction for Butler's strategy in *Bodies that Matter*. It does not involve promoting the affirmation of homosexuality and the abject of heterosexuality, as in a kind of Foucauldian reverse discourse, because this would involve sticking to the same logic that produced the abjection in the first place and would, if anything, reinstate heterosexuality. (Just as from Butler's perspective, Irigaray's strategy of establishing an alternative female imaginary would, in a sense, affirm the heterosexual imperative by keeping the duality of sexual difference and the male/female binary intact.)

In other words, Butler turns to psychoanalysis in *Bodies that Matter* in order to theorize the ways in which the body in its material reality comes into being as an object for ourselves, and as an object for others, through identificatory processes, and desire, that are structured by social and psychic regulation. This works through imaginary processes that are bound up with signification. She also wants to reveal the ways in which the heterosexual imperative shapes these imaginary processes and signification in order to denaturalize the whole process; and to further her argument that it makes no sense to think of the body as a stable referent outside of the process of its material-ization. Just as she wants to reject a distinction between a pro-cess of social construction and an object on which that process acts, she also wants to reject a distinction between the psyche and the body. It is not so much that there is a pre-existing body on which the process of identification acts, it is more that the body comes into being only through the process of identification.

Her point in regard to the materiality of the body, to reiterate, is not to suggest that bodies are immaterial. It is rather to stress the materiality of significations and the regulatory frameworks through which embodied subjects achieve cultural intelligibility (or not). Butler wants to reveal that not only are these shaped by a symbolic order that is both phallocentric and heterosexist, but also that this symbolic order *depends* for its stability on the exclusion and repudiation of the abject of heterosex. The route to change and transformation therefore becomes a matter of disrupting the workings of the heterosexual imperative that shapes the imaginary by denaturalizing it and reaffirming the abject of heterosex, with the aim of bringing the culturally unintelligible into the realm of intelligibility. This is the way to produce 'a potentially productive crisis' which will allow the possibility of 'reconfiguring the mapping of sexual difference' and allow the space for the emergence of an alternative, anti-heterosexist imaginary.

This, then, is a political strategy above all else, as she makes clear in an interview with Meijer and Prins (1998). It is also clearly a deconstructive strategy and is reminiscent of Derrida's critique of the metaphysics of presence.[11] The latter involves highlighting the instabilities involved in the production of logo-centric certainty in order to disrupt the logic on which it is based from within it. Butler employs a similar strategy in her attempt to find a way of disrupting and displacing the heterosexual imperative, which shapes these imaginary processes and also reifies the duality of sexual difference.[12] Furthermore, Butler aims to use these insights positively, as Derrida does, to develop alternative significations. The outcome, however, will not be determinable in advance.

However, the notion of producing a 'politically disruptive crisis' and the idea that the outcome of political strategies will not be determinable in advance do not sound very efficacious as political strategies to many feminists, especially those working in more sociological contexts. Opening up possibilities is not the same as actually achieving change, nor does it guarantee that the changes produced will be those that were sought. There is also some concern that the focus on the heterosexual imperative and the homosexual body as abject does not address the hierarchical relations involved in gender categories. Furthermore, this view of the materiality of the body has been criticized by feminists from a range of perspectives, united by a concern with the specificities of women's bodies and the significance of these in gender-based inequalities. (It has also been criticized by 'trans' theorists concerned with the materiality of transsexual bodies, which is discussed in Chapter 5.) There are two broad aspects to these concerns: one centres on the materiality of bodies in their corporeality; the other concerns the effects of sex/gender and heterosexuality as material structures.

Materiality and corporeality

One of the great strengths of Butler's account of performativity is that it shows that there is no *necessary* connection between the specificities of human bodies and the cultural frameworks through which they come into being – the process of signification through which embodied subjects achieve cultural intelligibility, or not. This is a valuable insight in denaturalizing the body and sex/gender categories and revealing the power relations, misogyny and homophobia involved in their construction. However, Butler's insistence on going further than that and refusing to allow the body *any* role in the process of its construction is much more problematic. What then becomes of the specificities of women's bodies and the relationship of these to our subjectivity, and to gender-based inequalities?

Butler's account is accused of 'losing its hold on the lived fleshy, experienced matter of (womanly) bodies' (Hughes and Witz 1997: 59) because her 'heavy reliance on the notion of citationality and its relation to the overarching influence of the heterosexual law works to occlude gendered corporeality behind the materialization of sexed bodies' (p. 59). This echoes the concerns of many theorists concerned with the connection between the materiality of the female body and gender-based inequalities. But the problem here lies in those very difficulties in establishing just what 'gendered corporeality' might mean, which are highlighted in Butler's work. To assume that this is something that exists in itself, outside cultural frameworks and signification, and is lived 'as such', as Hughes and Witz suggest, seems to invoke the possibility of some sort of unmediated experience, which is precisely what Butler is suggesting is *not* possible. There is no way of addressing the body 'as such' outside of our modes of conceptualization. This is not to say that the body is nothing, no-thing, that it has no matter outside language, precisely because, as discussed earlier, in Butler's account the two, matter and signification, are 'radically incommensurable'. Moreover, in her account, as in Derrida's, there is always an excess to signification. However, whilst matter is never fully captured in signification, and it is not reducible to signification, the two nevertheless remain indissociable. The crucial point is well made by Butler herself in the preface to *Bodies that Matter*:

> For surely bodies live and die; eat and sleep; feel pain; pleasure; endure illness and violence; and these 'facts' one might sceptically proclaim cannot be dismissed as mere construction. Surely there must be some kind of necessity that accompanies these primary and irrefutable experiences. And surely there is. But their irrefutability in no way implies what it might mean to affirm them and through what discursive means.
>
> (Butler 1993a: xi)

Clearly, it is not the body 'as such' that shapes our cultural frameworks but our cultural frameworks that shape the body 'as such'. Gender-based inequalities do not result from the specificities of women's (or men's) bodies as such, but from the ways in which their capacities are conceptualized; from the possibilities that the differential significations 'man' and 'woman' incorporate. These significations are themselves products of the interrelation of the various social imaginaries that regulate the materialization of the body.

Nevertheless, refusing to allow the body any role in the process of materialization remains problematic. It has been criticized by feminists who want to allow some sense of the specificities of women's bodies and thus make the body 'more of a drag on signification' (Martin 1994: 112); and also by trans theorists who want to accord the materiality of the 'lived body' some sort of causal role in the experience of transsexuality (Prosser 1998). The argument from both these perspectives is not that the body is not in some sense constructed, but rather that the materiality of the body does exert some kind of limit or constraint in the process of that construction. However, trans experiences are discussed in Chapter 5, so for now the focus remains on feminist critiques.

Martin attributes Butler's refusal to accord the body any kind of constraint to her focus on queer identity and is concerned that this is at the expense of feminist concerns with the specificities of women's bodies, and the role these play in gender-based inequalities. She argues that even if there is no way of getting at our bodily experiences outside of cultural frameworks and signification, it is still necessary to maintain a sense of the materiality of the body as some kind of limit. Otherwise 'the all-too-obvious and thus invisible difference that it makes to be a woman drops out of view' (Martin 1994: 112). Martin argues

> that we pay more respect to what's given, to limits, even as we open the future to what is now unthinkable or delegitimated, that we do this in order to generate a notion of difference that is not fixed or stable in its distribution across bodies, but is also not dispensable.
>
> (p. 112)

Butler's notion of constraint, however, only concerns the 'constitutive constraints' involved in the symbolic demand to take up sexed positions, and the repudiations and exclusions involved in this. It does not allow the consideration of the kind of constraints that Martin is suggesting, any more than it considers constraints that result from biological or physiological features. Furthermore, precisely because Butler refuses to accept a notion of sexual difference as immutable or irreducible, but rather socially instituted to function as such, she will not accept it as in some sense indispensable, as Martin suggests. This would be to continue the binary thinking that she wants to challenge. As she concedes in one interview, there is a limit to constructedness, but just what that limit is remains unspecifiable (Meijer and Prins 1998).

Does this then make her account inimical to feminist projects? Butler would argue against this view, and the view that feminist projects need to be based on the specificities of women's bodies, for all the reasons discussed already. Indeed, many feminists use her approach productively in their analyses of gender performativity and the practices of femininity and masculinity. However, this is not to deny that Butler's account of the body in *Bodies that Matter* does lack attention to the 'weightiness and constraints' that our bodily experience seems to impart (Alsop *et al.* 2002: 198). Alsop *et al.* examine this issue in relation to the bodily experiences of disabled women. They suggest that there is clearly a sense in which the experiences of disabled bodies are a product of particular conceptions of disability/ability which are reflected in social organization and public responses to disability and disfigurement, which are often negative. This aspect of disabled embodiment reveals the mediation of cultural frameworks in an individual's experience of their body as disabled, and indeed often abject, that is in keeping with Butler's account of performativity. Nonetheless, referring to Mairs (1997), who provides a lucid description of the experience of multiple sclerosis, Alsop *et al.* argue that the body also exerts a 'brute force' that is inescapable in terms of pain, incapacity and physical atrophy; and this sets a limit to the process of construction that is not accounted for in Butler's theory of performativity.

However, Butler does not incorporate a sense of brute force as Alsop *et al.* describe it in her account of performativity, as this would be something that it is not possible in this approach to contain. It could only be thought of in terms of an excess to signification. In any other sense, our understanding and experience of it would always be a product of our modes of signification because there is no way we could get outside them to the brute force itself, any more than we can have access to a body 'as such'. To reiterate an earlier point, 'there can be no reference to a pure materiality except via materiality' (Butler 1993a: 68). Even the irrefutability of bodily experiences such as pain, illness and death 'in no way implies what it might mean to affirm them and through what discursive means' (p. xi). This is not to say that any such brute force does not have any effects so much as to say that any effects it does have will always be mediated.

Butler does take up a second strand in Alsop *et al.*'s critique: that is, the issue of our attachments to particular bodily forms, and further develops her account of the affective relations in which we stand with our bodies in *The Psychic Life of Power* (1997b) and, to some extent, *Excitable Speech* (1997a). In *The Psychic Life of Power* she examines the way that power, understood as social regulation, produces and regulates the psychic aspects of identity, though a development of the notion of subjection. She argues that subjection involves both subordination to power and the production of 'passionate' attachments to identity categories, however insalubrious. This is discussed in Chapter 3. In *Excitable Speech*, which is discussed in Chapter 4, she develops these ideas in relation to 'hate speech', focusing in particular on homophobia in the military, pornography and racist hate speech.

The materiality of sex/gender and heterosexuality

However, it is not the corporeality of the body 'as such' that concerns another set of criticisms of Butler's account of the materiality of the body, but rather the neglect of gender and heterosexuality as social structures. It is claimed that Butler's attention to the materiality of the signifier lacks a materialist analysis that can address these aspects. One such criticism involves the view that not taking account of the biological basis of sex/gender neglects the systematic and structural nature of male power and domination (Ramazanoglu 1995). Another involves the view that it neglects the structural features involved in heterosexuality, 'the material and social relations which underpin the category of sex' (Jackson 1995: 17) as well as the exploitation of the bodies of women and their labour. Ebert (1996) also makes a related criticism from the perspective of a 'red feminism'. She argues that Butler's focus on the symbolic regime of heterosexuality, rather than the social formation of patriarchal capitalism as the determining structure, renders her account of performativity 'ludic': it neglects material social realities in favour of a focus on the superstructural play of discursive processes. In other words, Butler's analysis is accused of being confined to cultural and institutional aspects of social relations rather than the material conditions that produce them, such as patriarchy, capitalism, women's reproductive role, or a combination of these.

However, for Butler, these material conditions are themselves products of cultural frameworks (or imaginary schemata) and signification which, rather than merely reflecting the material conditions, instead *produce* them as causes, including economic relations, patriarchy, biology, sexuality and gender. Understanding the material entities that comprise social life and relations, whatever the focus, thus requires attention to the materiality of signification, which is articulated in practices. In relation to the body, it simply does not make sense to think of bodies or sex and gender outside of that significatory process as the source of oppression or inequality in a capitalist or patriarchal system, since the meaning of the body, and of those systems, can only ever be understood within signification. Change and transformation therefore need to be addressed through the significatory processes that produce the understanding of the materiality of the body and sex/gender as the source of those oppressions. Butler's emphasis on a genealogy of the body's materialization through the category of sex is a means of revealing the ways in which bodies are materialized in the service of a heterosexist norm; and of identifying the role of power and signification in this process.

Indeed, in an article in *New Left Review*, Butler addresses Marxist criticisms of her work as 'merely cultural' and neglecting economic factors in the context of a debate with Nancy Fraser. Butler points out that sex and sexuality are part of the relations of production and reproduction and, as such, are intrinsically related to the economic sphere, as much feminist work sought to establish in the 1970s and 1980s. She emphasizes that the realm of sexual production, conceived as part of the sexual division of labour, was located as part of the material conditions of life 'because normative gender serves the reproduction of the heterosexually normative family' (Butler 1998b: 40). Against Fraser she argues that struggles to transform the social field of sexuality do not become central to political economy to the extent that they can be directly tied to the question of unpaid and exploited labour, but also because they cannot be understood without an expansion of the 'economic sphere' itself to include both the reproduction of goods as well as the social reproduction of persons.

(p. 40)[13]

Ebert argues in her critique of Butler, in relation to the devaluing of female bodies in India, that 'no amount of resignification in the symbolic can change "what counts as a valued body", for what makes a body valuable in the world is its *economic value*' (Ebert 1996: 220, original emphasis). However, this does not take account of the way in which the economic value of bodies is itself discursively produced through cultural frameworks and signification (resulting in the social reproduction of persons). The lack of economic value of female babies, and the practice of aborting female foetuses due, in part, to the demand for large dowries when girls marry that Ebert cites, are all part of the enforced cultural performance of sexed and gendered bodies, which works through the production of individual identities via the incorporation of norms.

McNay (2000) also argues that Butler's focus on sexed identity neglects the asymmetry of gender hierarchies and fails to attend to the material and social factors as structural features. However, she says she does not want to imply a 'dualism where material struggles are seen as separable and prior to symbolic ones'. She argues that Butler is right to reject the kind of 'orthodox leftism' that relegates queer politics to an epiphenomenal concern with identity at the expense of more fundamental political concerns with redistribution. Indeed, she suggests that posing the cultural and material as oppositional could have the homophobic effect of excluding queer politics from the realm of real politics. Moreover, she also concedes that one of the strengths of Butler's account of performativity is that it recognizes the historicity of structure. In thinking her account of performativity through the psychoanalytic notions of identification and morphogenesis, Butler succeeds in reformulating the relation between the psyche and society; moreover, in thinking of

the symbolic in more social terms, as stabilized through citational practices, she does allow the possibility of resistance.
However, McNay (2000) argues that her success in this area is
limited by a lack of attention to the complex of power relations,
symbolic and material, which give rise to political action. Butler
still ultimately tends 'to privilege a symbolic account of subjectification over an examination of its material dimensions' (p. 47)
which results in 'a reduction of the broader issue of gender hierarchies to that of the construction of sexual identity' (p. 47). The
basis of McNay's concerns is that 'the idea of performativity
clearly alludes to the complex interplay of material and symbolic relations but does not really disaggregate them analytic-
ally' (p. 61). Butler's strategy for change thus remains at the level
of an abstract potentiality rather than a concrete possibility.
It does not, indeed cannot, predict when the destabilization of
hegemonic identifies will be successful, or which conditions will
result in the development of new identities.

The main deficiency in Butler's account, in McNay's analysis,
is that it does not provide a link between the symbolic or imaginary formulations and the material relations in which these
occur. McNay argues that this would involve a consideration of
the historical and social context to establish 'a logic of practice'
in order to determine when political action would be effective.
As a result of this omission, 'Butler's work often moves too
quickly from outlining the constitutive instability of symbolic
systems to claiming a political status for certain "excentric" sexual practices' (p. 61, citing Hennessey 1992). Furthermore, she
'underestimates the extent to which there can be a recuperation
of seemingly radical practices' (p. 59).

Butler, however, is well aware of the problem of the possibility
of recuperation as her analysis of *Paris is Burning* made clear
(see Chapter 1). The problem is that from her deconstructive
perspective, with its emphasis on the unpredictability of meaning, it is simply not possible to predict the effects of political
action in advance. Nor would the provision of a context to provide a 'logic of practice' fix the outcome in the way that McNay
suggests. This might be further illuminated when considering
the claim that Butler's focus on sexed identity neglects the
asymmetry of gender hierarchies.

Butler focuses on sexed identity because gender hierarchies

are a product of sexual difference as it is constituted in heterosexuality, and heterosexuality is regulated and governed by the
heterosexual imaginary. As she says in a debate with Benhabib,
Cornell and Fraser, which took place the same year that *Bodies
that Matter* was published: 'Neither the "masculine" nor the
"feminine" in his [Lacan's] sense can be sustained without the
presupposition of the structural asymmetry of heterosexuality'
(Butler 1995a: 142).[14] It is the structural asymmetry that regulates gender hierarchies that is the focus of Butler's concern in
her reformulation of performativity in *Bodies that Matter*.
In this reformulation, that which is intelligible is always constituted by what it excludes – 'the constitutive outside' – and this is
crucial to the forming of the symbolic as 'a limiting horizon'.
Therefore, the political project needs to move beyond an analysis of what is already given. Hence Butler's concern with the
abject, and that which is abject, which is not already compre-
hended, and which is not accounted for in the symbolic positions
articulated by Lacan. She asks:

> What does it mean to be 'outside' or 'beyond' the 'mascu-
> line' and the 'feminine'? That region is yet to be mapped but
> its mapping will demand a rethinking of the governing
> power of the symbolic as the heterosexualizing prerequisite
> by which the viability of the subject, masculine or feminine,
> is linguistically instituted.
>
> (Butler 1995a: 142)

This also relates to McNay's point about the problems of a
strategy that involves abstract potentialities rather than concrete
possibilities. In Butler's account of performativity it can be seen
that it is not always possible to specify the abject in a concrete
way, precisely because it is unthinkable, unrepresentable or
socially unintelligible. What is required, therefore, is to think
otherwise and, in particular in Butler's analysis, to reconceptual-
ize beyond the binary frame. Campaigning in terms of material
resources may be a necessary strategy for the acquisition of, say,
political rights for excluded or oppressed groups, but it will not
effect fundamental transformation because the logic that produced the exclusions in the first place would not be affected.
Whilst McNay highlights the problem that the possibility of

recuperation presents for Butler's strategy for change and transformation, Butler's deconstructive approach reveals that the way in which social change works is not predictable in advance. This means that setting the context to predict the outcome, as McNay suggests Butler's account needs to do, is simply not possible for the kinds of transformations that Butler suggests are required. For Butler, it is not just a question of juridical rights etc., but of rethinking the cultural framework that produced the abjection – in this case the heterosexual imaginary – the relative stability of which depends on their exclusion; and this is a much taller order.

Nevertheless, in highlighting these problems, McNay echoes the concerns of many feminist critics, and highlights what is often perceived to be a significant difficulty with Butler's approach for feminist political action: the inability to provide a programmatic vision (Webster 2000). This is a criticism that is typically made of deconstructive approaches, feminist and non-feminist, where the practical applicability of an avowed political stance is often far from apparent to those whose concerns are more obviously empirical. It is also a criticism that is very much disputed by those who employ a deconstructive approach, not by claiming that their work does provide a programmatic vision, but by articulating the difficulties with any such attempt. Indeed, this is a criticism with which Butler continues to grapple in much of her subsequent work as she continues to develop her account of performativity and the political possibilities it entails.

3   Performativity, subjection and the possibility of agency

Throughout Butler's work, she has maintained that the practices which constituted us as gendered subjects also provide the possibility of agency and resistance. In other words, she has tried to show that these practices are simultaneously constricting and enabling; or, as Moya Lloyd puts it, that '[g]ender is simultaneously a mechanism of constraint (a set of norms which define us as normal/abnormal) and a locus for productive activity' (Lloyd 1999: 200). In *The Psychic Life of Power*, this ambivalence is developed in the context of a theory of subjection, in which social power and regulation are in operation in the formation of the psyche, but which also allows for the possibility of resistance. It aims to show that the very process of becoming an intelligible human being involves a process of subjection that carries within it the possibility for resistance and change, despite involving psychological structures of subjectivity. The Foucauldian point that the very power that subjects us is also the source of our resistance is thus read psychoanalytically. It is argued that the process of subjection involves the operations of power in the formation of the psyche to produce 'passionate attachments' to identity categories that cannot be simply disregarded, as it is through these that we come into being. Nevertheless, it is also argued that the basis of these passionate attachments – this psychic regulation – is social and historical, and therefore contingent. This allows the possibility for change and transformation. In demonstrating the role of the social in the formation of the psyche, Butler thus aims to further address the issue of resistance, agency and resignification in her account of performativity whilst simultaneously addressing the problems of resistance that limit Lacanian and Foucauldian accounts of subject formation. She aims to theorize more effectively the Foucauldian claim that the power that produces us is not just external to us but part of us. It forms the basis of our existence and our possibilities even as it subjects us to its workings. In so doing, she is able to account for the intractability of identity categories without at the same time prohibiting the possibility of change: to render them 'durable but not immutable' as McNay puts it in another context.

This chapter explains and examines these moves in detail. It considers the implications of these developments for Butler's earlier work and focuses in particular on the political implications of this view of agency for feminist projects, including the claim that although Butler attempts to provide a means of understanding how the two aspects of the psyche and the social are in fact interrelated, her own account fails to accommodate the social (McNay 1999).

Subjection

> If, as Althusser implies, becoming a subject requires a kind of mastery indistinguishable from submission, are there perhaps political and psychic consequences to be wrought from such a founding paradox?
>
> (Butler, *The Psychic Life of Power*, p. 30)

> The desire for desire is exploited in the process of social regulation, for if the terms by which we gain social recognition for ourselves are those by which we are regulated and gain social existence, then to affirm one's existence is to capitulate to subordination – a sorry bind.
>
> (Butler, *The Psychic Life of Power*, p. 79)

After *Gender Trouble*, Butler becomes increasingly concerned with the psychic aspects of identity and the role of social regulation and power in the formation of the psyche. She becomes rather less satisfied with the relationship between interiority and exteriority in a Foucauldian framework that conceives of power in terms of surface inscriptions, and that rejects psychoanalysis and the idea of the psyche as aspects of the workings of juridical power (see for example Butler 1992b, 1993a). In the introduction to *Bodies that Matter*, she argues that what Foucault neglected in his rejection of psychoanalysis as the 'repressive hypothesis were the productive aspects of the regulation of desire in psychoanalytic theories; the ways in which "repression" operates as a modality of productive power' (1993a: 22).[1] In *The Psychic Life of Power* Butler returns to this point and develops it in the context of theories of subjection in the work of Nietzsche, Hegel and Althusser.

Butler rethinks Althusser's account of interpellation, in order to combine a Foucauldian theory of power with a psychoanalytic theory of the psyche. These moves enable her to show how power not only forms the subject in a Foucauldian sense, providing 'the conditions of possibility of its existence and the trajectory of its desire', but also to identify 'the specific mechanisms through which the subject is formed in submission' (Butler 1997b: 2). She points out that these are lacking in Foucault's account of subjection. She also returns to her argument in *Bodies that Matter* that, read psychoanalytically, the regulation of desire works through foreclosure, involving disavowals and repudiations, rather than repression as Foucault understood it. This is significant because: 'As foreclosure, the sanction works not to prohibit existing desires but to produce certain kinds of objects and to bar others from the field of social production' (p. 25). This then allows her to focus on the significance of the foreclosure of homosexual desire (in both cultural and individual terms) which was also left unaddressed in Foucault's own work on sex, sexuality and subjection. Indeed, Butler links this account of foreclosure to Foucault's notion of a regulatory ideal to suggest 'an ideal according to which certain forms of love become possible and others impossible' (p. 25).

Furthermore, although foreclosure in this sense works in a productive rather than repressive way, by shaping the sort of attachments that are possible, it does nevertheless also 'work on the basis of an originary violence' (p. 25). Thus Butler is able to identify a kind of violence that is integral to the coming into being of any subject. Moreover, this marks the subject as split within itself in both a Nietzschean and a Freudian sense 'in which power that at first appears external, pressed upon a subject, pressing the subject into subordination, assumes a psychic form that constitutes the subject's self-identity' (p. 3). This works through the double-bind of a subject turning back on itself, so that the subject is formed 'in tandem with the unconscious' (p. 7). This spilt then provides a source of resistance within the subject itself which, it is often argued, is lacking in Foucault's account of disciplinary power and the production of docile bodies as a matter of surface inscriptions. It suggests 'an inassimilable remainder' that not only haunts the production of 'continuous, visible and located' subjects (p. 29) but which also sets limits within the process of subjectification.

In *The Psychic Life of Power* the concern is with how this originary violence works through a process involving the 'psychic incorporation of norms'. This becomes a question of the workings of desire and subjection; of how the subjection of desire becomes the desire for subjection. It involves combining (i) Nietzsche's account of the formation of conscience as a matter of the will turning back upon itself as a matter of self-beratement; (ii) Freud's account of melancholia and the development of subjectivity through the repression (but not complete negation) of the libido in the unconscious; and (iii) aspects of the work of Hegel on desire and recognition, in particular, the idiosyncratic reading of the 'Lordship and Bondage' section of the *Phenomenology of Spirit* that she provided in *Subjects of Desire* (Butler 1987a). Reading together these three accounts of the workings of desire in the simultaneous production of subjects and subjection, leads to the view that 'there is no formation of the subject without a passionate attachment to subjection' (p. 67). Butler is thus able to identify desire as one of the mechanisms through which power and social regulation work in the process of subjection. Hence:

> A critical analysis of subjection involves: (1) an account of the way regulatory power maintains subjects in subordination by producing and exploiting the demand for continuity, visibility and place; (2) recognition that the subject produced as continuous visible and located is nevertheless haunted by an inassimilable remainder, a melancholia that marks the limits of subjectivation; (3) an account of the iterability of the subject that shows how agency may well

consist in opposing and transforming the social terms by which it is spawned.

(Butler 1997b: 29)

Furthermore, the desire for recognition, for 'continuity, visibility and place', is reinterpreted in linguistic terms because, it is argued, it is only through language that individuals become intelligible as subjects (p. 11). 'Individuals come to occupy the site of the subject (the subject emerges simultaneously as a site), and they become intelligible only to the extent that they are, as it were, first established in language' (pp. 10–11). Desire thus becomes the desire for existence and the route to this is through norms and social regulation that work through the establishment of primary dependencies on power and linguistic categories. Or, as she puts it in *Excitable Speech*:

> That one comes to 'be' through a dependency on the Other – an Hegelian, and indeed, Freudian postulation – must be recast in linguistic terms to the extent that the terms by which recognition is regulated, allocated, and refused are part of the larger social rituals of interpellation.
>
> (Butler 1997a: 26)

Hence, there is a primary, linguistic vulnerability to power and exploitation. '[T]he subject pursues subordination as the promise of existence . . . Subjection exploits the desire for existence, where existence is always conferred from elsewhere; it marks a primary vulnerability to the Other in order to be' (pp. 20–21). 'There is no way to protect against that primary vulnerability and susceptibility to the call of recognition that solicits existence, to that primary dependency on a language we never made in order to acquire a tentative ontological status' (p. 26).

In other words, it is only through being interpellated through linguistic categories that bodies/subjects come into social existence. This process inaugurates the being of anybody (any body) either as an intelligible body/being or as abjected, as she argued in *Bodies that Matter*. It is not simply a matter of recognition in the Hegelian sense of self-reflection and the negation of externality then, but rather that the 'call', the address in interpellation, renders recognition (or abjection) possible. It confers existence within the realms of possibility, the 'circuit of recognition' or, beyond it, in abjection.

Moreover, reading her account of interpellation through Hegel and Nietzsche allows Butler to argue that whilst it is through the process of interpellation that subjects come into being, this process does not involve a pre-existing subject who is interpellated, as Althusser's account would seem to imply. Hence she rejects Althusser's suggestion that it is the hailing, the call in the address (as in the example he provides of a policeman calling 'hey you') which causes the subject to turn, because this would seem to imply a pre-existing complicity with the law, as well as some kind of 'doctrine of conscience' (p. 109) and a pre-existing subject who does the turning. She argues instead that '[i]t is important to remember that the turn towards the law is not necessitated by the hailing; it is compelling in a less than logical sense, because it promises identity' (p. 108).

Gender and melancholia

In order to develop these points in relation to the performativity of gender, Butler links this account of the role of subjection in the production of subjectivity to the Freudian notion of melancholia and the concept of 'passionate attachment'. To do this she draws on Freud's suggestion in *The Ego and the Id* that melancholia is central to the formation of identifications that form the ego, 'which is first and foremost a bodily ego'. She explains that melancholia in a Freudian sense means 'the unfinished process of grieving' (p. 133), in which the ego identifies with the lost object in order to preserve it. Hence, 'identifications formed through unfinished grief are the modes in which the lost object is incorporated and phantasmatically preserved in and as the ego' (p. 132). The lost object is thus transformed from external to internal without being fully acknowledged in the process of melancholic incorporation. According to Freud, therefore, Butler argues: 'Melancholy is both the refusal of grief and the incorporation of loss' (p. 142).

In order to argue that gender is an effect of melancholic incorporation, the lost object becomes the lost object of sexual attachment and desire, which is necessary to the formation of gender identity in Freud's description of the Oedipal conflict.

Hence, Butler relates her account of melancholia to Freud's account of the establishment of masculinity and femininity in *Three Essays on Sexuality* (1905) (cited in Butler 1997b). She argues that in this account, masculinity and femininity are accomplishments established through the loss of certain sexual attachments in the Oedipal stage that are not avowed and not grieved, but are foreclosed as a possibility from the beginning. Butler suggests that these accomplishments could thus be understood in terms of the workings of a heterosexual melancholy:

> the melancholy by which a masculine gender is formed through the refusal to grieve the masculine as a possibility of love; a feminine gender is formed (taken on, assumed) through the incorporative fantasy by which the feminine is excluded as a possible object of love, an exclusion never grieved, but 'preserved' through heightened feminine identification.
>
> (Butler 1997b: 146)

As well as involving a prohibition on incest, Butler argues, heterosexual identity in Freud's account is therefore based on a pre-existing prohibition on homosexual desire, which results in the simultaneous repudiation and incorporation of homosexual identifications. Thus, unavowed loss is intrinsic to the formation of the gendered ego; precisely because it is unavowed it remains unacknowledged. To acknowledge it would be to undermine the very coherence of gendered subjectivity because the loss itself is intrinsic to the formation of gender identity. However, although it is lost, homosexual identification is not entirely eradicated. The desire for the mother is incorporated into the ego of the girl, and the desire for the father is incorporated into the ego of the boy, in the process of melancholic incorporation. The loss of desire for the 'opposite' sex that is necessary to the achievement of heterosexual gender identity is thus not entirely eliminated but is rather, in a sense, retained in the process of incorporation. Consequently, it remains to haunt it; hence, the tenuousness of heterosexual identity. Gendered subjectivity is thus achieved and maintained through a primary and continued submission to the (unacknowledged) operations of social power and regulation. These are crucial to the formation of the psyche and the continued existence of the subject who is passionately attached to them and who is indeed dependent on them for 'recognition, visibility, and place'.

Although she recognizes that not all experiences of gender fit the above formulation, Butler argues that this does not invalidate the basic argument in which 'Freud articulates a cultural logic in which gender is achieved and stabilized through heterosexual positioning and any threats to heterosexuality become threats to gender itself' (p. 136). The point is that heterosexuality is cultivated through prohibitions, one of which is homosexual attachment. Melancholia is the mechanism through which the psychic sphere is socially regulated according to established norms, and through which homosexual desire is retained as a source of guilt.

Indeed, Butler identifies two aspects in her analysis of melancholic identification in 'Melancholy Gender/Refused Identification' (in *The Psychic Life of Power*). One involves explaining the process through which the ego becomes gendered; the other involves examining the implications of this for life in 'a culture which can mourn the loss of homosexual attachment only with great difficulty' (p. 133). She says her work represents a cultural engagement with psychoanalysis and highlights the lack of a public language of grief for the great many deaths through AIDS, and the lack of conventions for acknowledging the loss of homosexual love. Butler suggests this is emblematic of heterosexist hegemony and the ungrievability of homosexual attachment. She thus describes the production of melancholy through the compulsory production of heterosexuality. Therefore, as well as understanding melancholia as a psychic matter in operation at the individual level, she also wants to understand it in terms of the workings of a social, regulatory power in a broader, cultural context. In this broader context, acknowledging the loss of same-sex love objects is also foreclosed from the beginning. There is thus a prohibition on homosexual love, which is culturally reiterated and ritualized:

> What ensues is a culture of gender melancholy in which masculinity and femininity emerge as traces of an ungrieved and ungrievable love; indeed, where masculinity and femininity within the heterosexual matrix are strengthened

through the repudiations that they perform. In opposition to a conception of sexuality which is said to 'express' a gender, gender itself is here understood to be composed of precisely what remains inarticulate in sexuality.

(p. 140)

In *The Psychic Life of Power*, Butler understands psychoanalysis to be linked with gender performativity and performativity to be linked with melancholia. This differs from her account of the psychic aspects of gender in *Gender Trouble*, where they were considered in a more Foucauldian way as performative productions of the enactment of gender; it was these performative productions that gave the appearance of interior fixity. Furthermore, in *The Psychic Life of Power*, as in *Bodies that Matter*, she wants to take from psychoanalysis the view that the performativity of gender involves disavowals and repudiations and that 'the opacity of the unconscious sets limits on the exteriorization of the psyche'. Hence, 'what is exteriorized or performed can only be understood by reference to what is barred from performance, what cannot and will not be performed' (pp. 145–6). Gender melancholia is thus linked to the practice of gender performativity in the sense that if gender is produced as an effect of melancholia, as ungrieved (and ungrievable) loss, then the performance of gender might be seen as the 'acting out' of unresolved grief, in the psychoanalytic sense of involuntary acts motivated by the unacknowledged grief and aggression. The 'acting out' that is produced by melancholia is thus clearly not voluntary. Since the unconscious plays a formative role in the construction of gender identity, it cannot be open to change through the wilful manipulation of the subject's conscious intentions. Hence, the issue of choice, and the possibility of gender identity involving some sort of everyday optionality that haunted *Gender Trouble*, recedes further still from the bounds of possibility, along with the spectre of voluntarism.[2]

Drag

These moves then have significant implications for the earlier view of drag, as Butler herself acknowledges (p. 145). In *Gender Trouble*, drag is taken to reveal the structure of gender as a matter of imitation, and to expose gender and heterosexuality as unstable, impossible and inessential ideals. By appearing to operate outside of the binary understanding of identity categories, the suggestion was that it could, perhaps, challenge them. From the point of view of melancholic incorporation, however, drag provides an allegory of heterosexual melancholia, and is also better understood as a sort of 'acting out' that is motivated by unacknowledged loss; a loss that is both refused and incorporated and, as such, remains as the 'inassimilable remainder' to what is 'visible, continuous and located'. It also reveals 'the mundane psychic and performative practices by which heterosexualized genders form themselves through renouncing the possibility of homosexuality, a foreclosure that produces both a field of objects and a domain of those whom it would be impossible to love' (p. 146). Although the concern with instability continues, the understanding of the production of stability in more psychoanalytic terms is a significant shift, with significant political implications (which are discussed below).

In terms of the 'never-never' structure of the logic of repudiation at the heart of heterosexual melancholy, Butler acknowledges that her argument is somewhat hyperbolic: 'a logic in drag, as it were which overstates the case' (p. 149). Indeed, as she points out earlier, it leads to the conclusion that 'the "truest" lesbian melancholic is a straight woman, and the "truest" gay male melancholic is a straight man' (p. 147). In this formulation: 'The straight man becomes the man he never loved and never grieved; the straight woman becomes the woman she never loved and never grieved' (p. 147). However, Butler says that the reason for this overstatement is that she wants to emphasize the point that there is no necessary reason for identification and desire to be oppositional and to involve this form of repudiation. Indeed, 'We are made all the more fragile under the pressure of such rules and all the more mobile when ambivalence and loss are given dramatic language in which to do their acting out' (p. 150). This questioning of the separation of identification and desire continues an important theme in her critique of psychoanalytic theories that was present in *Gender Trouble* and her early critique of the heterosexualizing imperative in the work of both Freud and Lacan. She argued that the separation of identification and desire that is foundational to

Freud's account of Oedipal elations, and Lacan's linguistic reformulation of this in the mirror stage, is based on a hetero-sexual understanding of desire that assumes such a separation. So, whilst their accounts purport to explain gender and sexual-ity, those explanations are themselves based on normative heterosexuality.[3]

Political implications

Butler's central point in this account of subjection through interpellation and melancholic incorporation, in the series of readings in *The Psychic Life of Power*, is that the power that produces us is not just external to us but part of us. It forms the basis of our existence even as it subjects us to its workings. It is the source of our possibilities even as it ensures our subjection. The source of our subjection is therefore also the source of our agency. This, then, as Butler herself admits, 'can hardly be the basis for an optimistic view of the subject or of a subject centred politics' (p. 29). Nevertheless, a guiding theme in the develop-ment of her account of psychic subjection concerns the political possibilities that it entails and the implications of these for a theory of agency.

The political question thus becomes: 'How to take an oppos-itional relation to power that is, admittedly, implicated in the very power one opposes' (p. 17). This is, of course, the question that ultimately dogged Foucault's work, as discussed earlier. Butler tries to answer it in *The Psychic Life of Power* by focus-ing on the psychic aspect of power to show how the power that is formative of the psyche is *social* in origin and so open to resistance and change. Although the route to change and trans-formation continues to be through resistance and resignifica-tion, the point now is that the foreclosures, exclusions and disavowals that operate through the psyche to form identity are social in origin, and thus contingent, politically motivated and, most importantly, historically revisable.

This focus on the role of the social in the formation of the psychic aspects of identity allows Butler to acknowledge the importance of the unconscious in the formation of identity, without losing sight of the role of the social in the formation of the unconscious, as both Freud and Lacan are accused of doing.[4]

Indeed, she develops what McNay (1999, 2000) describes as a 'sociocentric' conception of the psyche that involves a refusal of the distinction between the psyche and the social that is a consequence of Lacan's separation of the symbolic and the imaginary.

This is important for Butler's critique of Lacan and for feminist appropriations of his work. In dissolving the separation of the symbolic and the imaginary in Lacan's tripartite structure, Butler is able to address one of the main problems that concern feminists who draw on his work. This concerns the apparent inability in a Lacanian framework to reformulate the symbolic in other than patriarchal terms (as the law of the father). It is argued that although Lacan's account of the symbolic and the imaginary can provide useful insights about the role of language and signification in the production of gendered subjectivity, his distinction between the psyche and the social, the symbolic and the empirical historical realm, deprives it of a means to challenge existing social relations (Braidotti 1991). (This would include what Butler describes as 'heterosexual hegemony'.) Butler's more sociocentric conception of the psyche provides a way of understanding how these two aspects are in fact interrelated and so provides a way around this impasse. It allows her to emphasize the political aspects of identification and, crucially, to acknowledge that the unconscious not only sets limits on the kinds of identifications that are possible, but that these limits are themselves the products of power relations that operate through social regulation. Butler's Foucauldian reading of the psyche as a product of social regulation allows her to identify the mechanisms through which this works (i.e. foreclosure, the psychic incorporation of norms, and melancholia). Hence, as McNay puts it, the strength of Butler's 'sociocentric concept of the psyche is the extent to which it can explain the non-correspondence between hegemonic gender norms and sexuality in terms other than pre-social imaginary identifications which leave the symbolic intact as an immutable law' (McNay 1999: 186). In so doing, it also avoids the tendency to privilege the psyche over the social, which often remains a stumbling block in attempts to adapt a Lacanian framework to accommodate feminist concerns (e.g. Brennan 1993; Cornell 1993).

Moreover, Butler's account of melancholic incorporation

provides important insights about the social and political nature of identification that clearly go some way to explaining the intractability of identity. Sexed identity becomes more clearly a 'durable but not immutable phenomenon' (McNay 2003: 139) Not only do these moves thus further rebut voluntarist interpretations of Butler's work, but they also address some of the difficulties inherent in other social constructionist accounts that fail to account for the intractability of identity categories and/or the contingency of the social, as McNay argues. The reformulation of the relationship between the psychic and the social, emphasizing the role of the social in psychic subjection, and the development of passionate attachments, both 'limits the contingency of the social' and the 'open-ended-ness of identity' (McNay 1999: 187). It also avoids the either/or of 'the dichotomy of fixity and contingency that hampers debates on identity'. In this sense, it 'pushes a feminist understanding of gender identity on to a new terrain' (p. 187).

Butler's theory of psychic subjection also further develops her theory of resistance. As Matisons argues, one problem with the notion of agency in *Gender Trouble* and *Bodies that Matter* is that 'the need to resignify remains underdeveloped' (Matisons 1998: 23). The account of the instability of bodily categories such as sex and gender is based on the view that they are normative ideals that are impossible to fulfil, and it is the 'the gap between the norm and its fulfilment that inevitably leads to a subjective need for resignifications' (p. 23). However, Matisons argues, Butler does not provide a theory of agency or desire to explain where this subjective need comes from in either of these two works, whereas the turn to Freud and melancholia, and Hegel and desire in *The Psychic Life of Power*, addresses this problem: 'A desire prone to stubborn attachments is where the need comes from' (p. 25). Desire's dual aspects of a capacity to withdraw and reattach and the goal of the continuation of the self, are the source of resistance and the possibility of resignification; these primary features of desire provide the basis for the theory of resistance. Alternatively, as Lloyd puts it: 'Paradoxically, it is the trauma of subjection that, psychoanalytically, allows for the reworking or resignifying these painful interpellations . . . the potential for reiteration can unsettle the mode of attachment such that subject reformation can go ahead' (Lloyd

1998: 39). The space for change is thus theoretically defined in Butler's reworking of Oedipal relations in terms of melancholic incorporation in *The Psychic Life of Power*. The identifications, avowals and disavowals through which we become viable subjects or not, with intelligible or unintelligible bodies, have a degree of fluidity: they are not fixed and permanent, even as they cannot simply be cast aside. In this sense, 'resistant forms of identification, although constituted in the same field as power relations, would appear to have the potential to contest, maybe even to subvert, dominant norms of gender' (p. 40).

Agency and political practice

There seems little doubt that Butler's account of the psychic life of power does leave the theoretical space for change and the possibility of resistance. What is much more problematic, however, is the question of how to operationalize the political possibilities, given the significance of the unconscious and the role of disavowals and exclusions in the constitution of identity; and the theory of agency involved in Butler's account of politics as a matter of identification and resistance to interpellation. Although Butler's work provides significant insight into the political nature of identification, these same insights also pose problems for designing a politics around identification and commonality. As Diana Fuss argues:

> Perhaps the most serious difficulty with designing a politics around identification is the fact that the unconscious plays a formative role in the production of identifications, and it is a formidable (not to say impossible) task for the political subject to exert any steady or lasting control over them. Given the capacity of identifications continually to evolve and change, to slip and shift under the weight of fantasy and ideology, the task of harnessing a complex and protean set of emotional ties for specific social ends cannot help but pose intractable problems for politics.
>
> (Fuss 1995: 9–10)

Furthermore, as Lloyd argues, if 'our social ties are not only with those with whom we consciously identify, but are constructed through a disallowed dependence on those we unconsciously reject, then commonality – or identity – as the basis of our political affiliations is challenged' (Lloyd 1998: 38). We need to appreciate the significance of non-identity, in our identifications, as well as identity.

This latter is of course one of the arguments that Butler has been making since *Gender Trouble*. As Diana Fuss puts it: 'Butler's work provides not a simple endorsement of the proliferation of identificatory possibilities but a considered evaluation of the ways in which any identification is purchased through a set of constitutive and formative exclusions' (Fuss 1995: 9). In *The Psychic Life of Power* this basic approach is reinterpreted in psychological terms so that those exclusions and repudiations become a matter of foreclosure and melancholic incorporation.

The political project thus become a matter of investigating 'what kinds of identifications are made possible, are fostered and compelled, within a given political field, and how certain forms of instability are opened up within that political field by virtue of the process of identification itself' (Butler 2000b: 150). It also becomes a question of reworking the injurious interpellations through which we come into being because: 'Called by an injurious name I come into social being. Inevitable attachment to existence leads me to embrace the terms that injure me because they constitute me socially' (Butler 1997b: 104). Nevertheless precisely because of the possibility of resistance and resignification in her account of subjection:

> This is not the same as saying that such an identity will remain always and forever rooted in its injury as long as it remains an identity, but it does imply that the possibilities of resignification will rework and unsettle the passionate attachment to subjection without which subject formation – and re-formation – cannot succeed.
>
> (p. 105)

One way to rework these 'injurious interpellations', Butler suggests, is to inhabit the social categories through which we are constituted in unintended ways, and in so doing to challenge and change their meaning. She provides examples of this in *Excitable Speech* in the context of a discussion of the performativity

of 'hate speech' and the limitations of relying on legal regulation
and censorship to combat it, with particular reference to racism
as well as sexism and homophobia. (These are discussed in
Chapter 4.)

Agency, then, becomes a matter of reworking injurious interpellations, of unsettling passionate attachments to subjection.
Its roots are not to be found in the structure of the subject and
autonomous action, which this view of power exposes as an
illusion (as discussed in Chapter 1), but in the workings of
power in the simultaneous production of subjects and subjection. They are to be found in the combined operations of social
power and psychic regulation and in the possibility of resistance
and resignification.

However, allowing the possibility for resistance and resignification does not necessarily mean that resistance will be successful, nor does it guarantee that the changes produced will be
those that are sought after, as discussed in Chapter 2 in connection with critiques of Butler's view of the materiality of the
body. Therefore, although this view of agency does provide a
certain amount of optimism in relation to Butler's own project
in *The Psychic Life of Power*, it does nothing to address the
difficulties raised by feminists concerned with concrete programmes of social change that were discussed in the previous
chapter.

As McNay argues, although Butler's rethinking of the relationship between the psyche and social demonstrates the limits
to the contingency of gender identity and, in demonstrating the
instability of the symbolic and signification, theoretically allows
the potential for change, her account of agency remains 'a predominantly negative one' (McNay 1999: 187) as it revolves
around the possibility of displacement and resignification.
Hence: 'The subject's relation to the socio-symbolic is conceived, by and large, in terms of negativity or constraint, which
. . . results in a tendency to valorize the act of signification per
se' (p. 187). In other words, it involves too much emphasis on
resistance and not enough on the creativity of human action.
Thus, Butler's account 'fails to draw out fully . . . the ways in
which the symbolic realm is composed of conflicting values and
resources which may be actively, and sometimes, creatively,
appropriated by actors to institute new value systems and new

forms of collective identity' (p. 187). So, although Butler is at pains to historicize the Lacanian notion of the symbolic, so that the law of the father that shapes it becomes hegemonic rather than immutable, McNay argues that her own work could be accused of 'running the risk of dehistoricizing the idea of performative agency' because the potential for change is located in 'the permanent disjunction between the psyche and the social' (p. 187). Furthermore, precisely because her account is lacking a more active concept of agency, 'Butler could be said to be vulnerable to her own criticism of the concept of the unconscious: resignification becomes a self-identical principle which forecloses an analysis of the variable nature of social action and change' (p. 187).

McNay argues that although Butler's account of performativity could address these issues, her account of the relationship between the psyche and the social in *The Psychic Life of Power* (and *Excitable Speech*) does not allow her to do so. She argues that: 'Butler needs to explain in more detail how symbolic norms relate to other social and political structures through which gender identities are also fashioned' (p. 191). Hence, McNay's main criticism of the political possibilities of Butler's account of identity formation is that it involves a politically debilitating emphasis on an individualistic conception of political practice as a matter of displacement and resistance. It thus lacks a means of engaging collectively with historical specificity.

Response to McNay

There are two particular problems with the idea of collective engagement with historical specificity from the point of view of performativity and subjection. One is to do with the limitations of working within existing frameworks – with that which is already given (i.e. the historically specific present). This can, and all too often does, result in co-option to existing power relations and regulatory ideals rather than actually challenging them or their basic premises. It does not provide a means of addressing the disavowals and repudiations which are denied expression in those existing frameworks – indeed on which those frameworks in fact depend – other than in the terms of the existing framework. For example, liberal political aims of granting women formal equality before the law do not engage with the disavowals and aggression on which masculine identity is based. The other problem concerns the creativity of human action. In Butler's account of *The Psychic Life of Power*, the creativity of human action is constrained by foreclosure, disavowals, repudiations and the psychic regulation of desire.

It might be useful to consider these matters in the context of Butler's debate with Laclau and Žižek about the nature of foreclosure in *Contingency, Universality, Hegemony* (Butler *et al.* 2000). Especially, Butler's response to Žižek's suggestion that she herself is a closet formalist 'relying on a silent proto-Kantian distinction between form and content' (Žižek 2000: 109) in her reading of Lacan's account of sexual difference as an ahistorical bar (in 'Competing Universalities', Butler 2000b).[5]

Žižek criticizes Butler (and Laclau) for conflating two levels of analysis: 'the need to distinguish more explicitly between contingency/substitutability *within* a certain historical horizon and the more fundamental exclusion/foreclosure that *grounds this very horizon*' (Žižek 2000: 108, original emphasis). Hence Butler's claim, against Lacan, that the exclusions through which subjects are constituted are 'politically salient, not structurally static' conflates 'the endless political struggle of/for inclusions/exclusions *within* a given field (say of today's late capitalist society) and a more fundamental exclusion which sustains this very field (p. 108, original emphasis). In relation to sexual difference, therefore, this is not fixed in a Lacanian framework, as Butler seems to suggest in her critique of Lacan, but 'the name of a deadlock, of a trauma, of an open question of something that resists every attempt at its symbolization' (pp. 110–11). Žižek argues this is thus far from a form of Kantian formalism. Indeed: 'Every translation of sexual difference into a set of symbolic opposition(s) is doomed to fail, and it is this very "impossibility" that opens up the terrain of the hegemonic struggle for what "sexual difference" will mean' (p. 111). Furthermore, he goes on: 'What is barred is *not* what is excluded under the present hegemonic regime' (p. 111, original emphasis). This is precisely because of the gap between the Real and its translation into symbolic operations.

For Žižek therefore, 'the historical horizon appears to exist on a different level from a more fundamental one, one which pertains to the traumatic lack in or of the subject' (Butler 2000b: 141). However, Butler rejects this separation of levels because, in her account, the symbolic *is* the idealization of dominant social and political structures. It is not that there is a Real that comes into being through translation into symbolic operations but is separable from them, it is rather that the very frameworks through which subjects come into being are part and parcel of that becoming (including even, *contra* Lacan and Žižek, any apparent structural or pre-social sexual difference). So, although 'every subject emerges on the condition of foreclosure' (p. 140), these foreclosures are social in origin and are 'not explicable through anachronistic structuralist accounts of kinship' (p. 140), whether in terms of the incest taboo and Oedipal relations, castration, or indeed sexual difference itself (whatever that may be).[6] Rather, the structures that govern the process of symbolization, the symbolic order, are contingent norms that seem to have ossified as psychic ideals. Indeed, this is Butler's crucial point and it is this that marks the difference of her approach from other psychoanalytic accounts. Although no subject emerges without certain foreclosures, she wants to reject 'the presumption that those constituting foreclosures, even traumas, have a universal structure that happened to be described perfectly from the vantage point of Lévi-Strauss or Lacan' (p. 148). So against Žižek's distinction between a fundamental level and a secondary social level, Butler says: 'I would suggest that those foreclosures are not secondarily social, but that foreclosure is a way in which variable social prohibitions work' (p. 149). It is not that they simply serve to constrain certain objects after they emerge, it is more that they 'constrain in advance the kinds of objects that can and do appear within the horizon of desire' (p. 149). Hence:

> Precisely because I am committed to a hegemonic transformation of this horizon, I continue to regard this horizon as a historically variable schema or episteme, one that is transformed by the emergence of the non-representable within its terms, one that's compelled to reorientate itself by virtue of the radical challenges to its transcendentality presented by 'impossible' figures at the borders and fissures of its surface.
>
> (p. 149)

In Butler's account of the melancholic incorporation of norms through the operations of foreclosure, the fundamental structural aspects of the symbolic or symbolization and the variable contingency of the historical become inseparable. Furthermore, historical specificity is significant in as much as it is the source of particular foreclosures. However, since foreclosures 'constrain in advance the kinds of objects that can and do appear', it is not enough to engage with historical specificity as currently given to effect change and transformation. It is necessary to address the question of what is not currently possible – hence her frequent references to Wittgenstein on the limits of conceptualization, and to any given formulation of sociality, in 'Competing Universalities'. She insists that 'we encounter this limit at various liminal and spectral moments in experience' (p. 152). For Butler, the point is that the opportunity to articulate these foreclosures is the first step in the process of rearticulation.

In a sense then, Butler is articulating a need for change in the conditions of possibility in the horizon of desire (which is structured by normative heterosexuality and associated kinship relations). This kind of change is not something that can be predicted in advance, precisely because it is as yet unthought. In terms of historical specificity, Butler is more concerned with the ways in which concrete political struggles are shaped by the foreclosures that inaugurate subjectivity, than accepting any apparent specificity as the cause of action. She emphasizes that is not just an individual matter as that would turn politics into a form of clinical psychoanalysis, it is rather a question of investigating 'what kinds of political identifications are made possible, are fostered and compelled, within a given political field, and how certain forms of instability are opened up within that political field by virtue of the process of identification itself' (p. 150). She gives the example of a 'shiny, new gay citizen' who wants to work in the military and have the opportunity to marry which, she argues, gives testimony to the multiplicity of identifications and undermines identity as 'a taken-for-granted set of interlocking positions' (p. 150). Hence:

> If the interpellation of the shiny, new gay citizen requires a
> desire to be included within the ranks of the military and to
> exchange marital vows under the blessing of the state, then

the dissonance opened up by this very interpellation opens up in turn the possibility of breaking apart the pieces of this suddenly conglomerated identity.

(p. 150)

However, although this might allow an alternative hegemonic formation to develop, there is no guarantee that it will. The point is that the categories that shape possible identifications serve a dual purpose. Whilst, on the one hand, they restrict in advance the 'play of hegemony, dissonance and rearticulation' (p. 150), at the same time they may 'become, with luck, the site for a disidentificatory resistance' (p. 151).

In relation to the question of agency, Butler says:

> In the intersection of Foucault and Freud I have sought to provide a theory of agency that takes into account the double workings of social power and psychic reality and this project, partially undertaken in *The Psychic Life of Power*, is motivated by the inadequacy of the Foucauldian theory of the subject to the extent that it relies upon either a behaviourist notion of mechanically reproduced behaviour or a sociological notion of 'internalization' which does not appreciate the instabilities that inhere in identificatory practices.

(p. 151)

From this Foucauldian perspective, the subject cannot be the ground of agency precisely because its very existence is a product of power relations, which 'delimit in advance what the aims and expanse of agency will be' (p. 151). Butler suggests that this does not mean that resistance is futile, however, 'that we are always-already-trapped' (p. 151). 'What it does mean, however, is that we ought not to think that by embracing the subject as the ground of agency, we will have countered the effects of regulatory power' (p. 151). This view neglects the phantasmatic dimension of social norms and interpellations: the ways in which the normative operations of social power work psychically to produce and sustain phantasmatic attachments to ideals that are simultaneously social and psychic. And that this involves a process of incorporation, or embodiment that is a sort of 'mode of interpretation', which is not necessarily conscious, as in the process of identification, 'which subjects normativity itself to an iterable temporality. Norms are not static entities, but incorporated and interpreted features of existence that are sustained by the idealizations furnished by fantasy' (p. 152). Which is why the analysis of psychic life is necessary: social norms are not simply internalized, unmediated, as in a sociological model, they require the activization of fantasy to produce 'phantasmatic attachment'. Moreover, Butler cautions against viewing this process as involving different levels of analysis: sociological and psychological as this would not address the way that 'social normativity is not finally thinkable outside the psychic reality which is the instrument and source of its continuing electivity' (p. 152)

So one might ask whether it is fair to claim that Butler's account

> fails to draw out fully . . . the ways in which the symbolic realm is composed of conflicting values and resources which may be actively, and sometimes, creatively, appropriated by actors to institute new value systems and new forms of collective identity.
>
> (McNay 1999: 188)

These conflicting values and resources make up the field of the already represented. Whereas, what Butler's account is trying to highlight is the ways in which the symbolic works to foreclose 'other', alternative representations, the unthought. Her particular focus is on the role of normative heterosexuality and the kinship relations it gives rise to in prescribing what will and will not be an intelligible life, a life worth living. So, although she recognizes the need to engage in the concrete struggles of, for example contemporary social movements, she is also wary of the ways in which these concrete struggles can be co-opted by existing institutions of power. Her emphasis on foreclosure aims to expose these, along with the 'contingency and risk intrinsic to political practice' (Butler 2000b 158).

Butler provides a number of examples of this, such as the feminist anti-pornography movement in the USA whose cause was co-opted by rightwing politicians. She also discusses the lesbian and gay movement and the gains made in relation to the inclusion of gay people in the US military and the extension of marriage rights to gay couples in some parts of Europe and the USA. Although these moves would seem to be positive gains in granting equal rights to non-heterosexuals, and would seem to be a positive sign of social inclusion, at the same time she warns that 'the granting of these questionable rights and obligations for some lesbian and gays establishes norms of legitimation that work to remarginalize others and foreclose possibilities for sexual freedom which have also been long-standing goals of the movement' (p. 160). Such gains do nothing to challenge the association of those rights and entitlements with the institution of marriage in the first place. 'So, the claim to extend the "right" of marriage to non-heterosexual people may appear at first to be a claim that works to extend existing rights in a more universalizing direction' but in effect it also serves to widen 'the gap between legitimate and illegitimate forms of sexual exchange' (pp. 176–7). Butler gives the example of single mothers and fathers, divorcees, lesbian gay and transgender people, and others who do not live monogamous lives, 'whose sexuality and desire do not have the conjugal home as their (primary) venue, whose lives are considered less real or less legitimate, who inhabit the more shadowy regions of social reality' (p. 176).

In this sense then, the only way to produce 'a radical democratization of legitimating effects' would be to take marriage out of the equation as a source of legal entitlement. Capitulating to either side in debates about inclusion involves the furtherance of state power and the hegemony of institutionalized heterosexuality, as well as the foreclosure of other possibilities as intelligible or worthwhile modes of living and relating. What is required instead is to displace that culture: this is Butler's aim.[7] Furthermore, she insists, 'it should become clear that I am not, in this instance, arguing for a view of political performativity which holds that it is necessary to occupy the dominant norm in order to produce an internal subversion of its terms' (p. 177). This would be the case in a politics of parody as suggested in *Gender Trouble*:

> Sometimes it is important to refuse the terms, to let the term itself wither, to starve it of it strength. And there is, I believe, a performativity proper to refusal, which in this instance

insists upon the reiteration of sexuality beyond the dominant terms. What is subject to reiteration is not 'marriage' but sexuality, forms of intimate alliance and exchange, the social basis for the state itself.

(p. 177)

What Butler is doing, then, is providing a theoretical account of the conditions of possibility for the political, and for change and transformation; and at the same trying to demonstrate the inadequacies of divorcing the symbolic from concrete empirical reality, as the symbolic is, and can only ever be, instantiated in the concrete. It thus makes no sense to think of it in terms of universal structures (as in her disagreement with Lacan and Žižek on the issue of sexual difference, discussed above, and other psychoanalytic accounts of the Oedipal conflict and castration complex).[8] She is attempting to provide a means of theorizing gender practices as sites of critical (i.e. resistant) agency, whilst simultaneously recognizing their implication in power relations, and the regulatory ideals of normative heterosexuality (which produce and sustain heterosexual hegemony). Further to this, and crucially, she is concerned with the possibility of 'hegemonic rearticulation', with the question of 'how to grasp the dynamism of hegemonic rearticulation' (Butler *et al.* 2000: 271). The account of 'the social' involved is not abstract because it is concerned with the performativity of social norms as embodied and reiterated. 'Moreover, it offers a perspective on embodiment, suggesting that knowledge, to the extent that it is embodied as habitus (Bourdieu), represents a sphere of performativity that no analysis of political articulation can do without' (p. 270). In relation to the politics of gender, 'the embodied performativity of social norms will emerge as one of the central sites of political contestation' (p. 270). So, in that sense, it is not so much that there is a problem with the level of analysis, as Žižek and McNay, amongst others, argue: the level of analysis is and must be the social. The problem is that Butler's understanding of the social involves recognition of the role of the inter-implication of the psyche, the symbolic and signification, in our experience of it. Indeed, this is her crucial point and it is this which makes her analysis original, even as it makes political projects based on her work 'difficult and risky'.

In this sense, it is difficult to justify the claim that 'resignification becomes a self-identical principle which forecloses an analysis of the variable nature of social action and change' as McNay proposes (cited above). This would be to suggest that resignification is somehow divorced from the concrete world of social action (or performative practice in Butler's terminology) when in fact the opposite is the case. It is rather that Butler's account attempts to address the question of how, if social action is as much a product of power and social regulation as it is a product of individual intentions, indeed if those very individual intentions along with self-identity and desires are products of social power and regulation, existing regimes of power and social regulation can be challenged; and transformation and change become possible. That this becomes a matter of signification and resignification is not capitulation to an abstract principle since, for Butler, 'the sign must always be situated within discursive practices' (p. 271); and discursive practices involve the iteration and reiteration of (gender) norms. The focus on foreclosure is a way of getting at the absences that structure discourse and performative practice.

Hence, politics must address the foreclosures involved in the psychic incorporation of norms because the articulation of the foreclosure provides the basis of the possibility for rearticulation, 'for the articulation can become rearticulated and countered once it is launched into a discursive trajectory, unmoored from the intentions by which it is animated' (p. 158). Since foreclosure is one of the mechanisms through which cultural intelligibility is produced through the exclusion of certain possibilities 'giving discursive form to the foreclosure can be an inaugurating moment of its destabilization' (p. 158). In this sense, then, it is not so much that it is an abstract potentiality that is identified by Butler, as a concrete possibility. The political possibilities of Butler's account of foreclosure and melancholic incorporation in the *Psychic Life of Power* are clearly not abstract in the sense of being divorced from the concrete world of performative action. However, they are abstract in the sense that they still do not do not provide a programmatic vision on which to base political action, as discussed in Chapter 2, but instead further demonstrate the difficulties with any such approach.

4 The politics of the performative

Hate speech, pornography and 'race'

There has been much debate in the US legal system around the role of the state in the regulation of 'hate speech'. At the heart of these debates is the conflict between the First and Fourteenth Amendments to the US Constitution. The former provides for freedom of speech and the latter for freedom from harm from the conduct of others. The main concern of the courts is to establish whether hate speech is a form of conduct. If so, government intervention to restrict it is legitimated. However, if it is established that the hate speech in question is only a matter of words, then it becomes an expression of free speech and intervention to restrict it would contravene the First Amendment. It would seem then that speech act theory could provide a useful resource through which to argue for the regulation of hate speech. The grounds would be that it exerts a performative force which constitutes an injury and therefore should be regarded as conduct, or action, rather than the mere expression of a viewpoint.

In *Excitable Speech*, subtitled *The Politics of the Performative*, Butler takes issue with the portrayal of hate speech in this way in relation to the regulation of racist hate speech, declarations of homosexuality in the US military, and pornography. It may at first sight seem strange that she should do so, given the emphasis on the role of language in the constitution of subjectivity, identity and the materiality of the body in her own theory of performativity. However, if it is recalled that the basic premise that underlies all of Butler's work is that we are in some sense linguistically constituted, but that it does not follow from this that we are also linguistically *determined*, this stance becomes less surprising. In her account of performativity it is precisely because speech acts are 'excitable' – i.e. their meanings and effects are out of the control of the speaker and so cannot be fixed by either their intentions or their authority – that there is always the possibility for the speech act to perform alternative meanings to those that are expressly intended. In *Excitable Speech* Butler explores the possibilities for resistance that stem from this excitability in relation to hate speech. Her analysis suggests that this may be a less risky and more fruitful course of action than challenging the workings of hate speech through state legislation.

Moreover, one of the purposes of examining the relationship between speech and action as it is conceived in the hate speech debates is for Butler to further her theoretical project by elaborating on the *ways* in which subjects may be constituted in discourse, but yet could also appropriate the discourses which constitute them in non-conventional ways. Just as in *Gender Trouble* and *Bodies that Matter*, the aim was to demonstrate that the practices through which we become gendered subjects are simultaneously (and paradoxically) the location of regulation and constraint, and agency and resistance; and in *The Psychic Life of Power* she aims to show that the power that subjects us is also the source of our agency. In *Excitable Speech* she aims to show how the operations of hate speech 'do not destroy the agency required for a critical response' (Butler 1997a: 41) but rather provide the possibility for such agency – precisely because of the citational, temporal nature of speech acts, including those that are injurious.

Indeed, it is her focus on this possibility that is at the root of her disagreement with the hate speech advocates. Furthermore, at the root of her view of this potential is her anti-humanism and rejection of the notion of sovereign power which, in her analysis, underpins the arguments of the hate speech proponents. She argues that they grant too much determinism and too much power to the words to 'wound'. They do not provide enough recognition of the enabling aspects of speech acts, however injurious. Language has the power to enable social existence and to injure, and in this sense there is a kind of 'linguistic vulnerability' at the heart of subjectivity, but this very vulnerability carries within it the possibility for resistance.[1] In order to show this, Butler sets her analysis of the uses of speech act theory in the US legal system in the context of a discussion about what it means to say that language has the power to injure. This involves a further engagement with Austin's account of speech act theory and Althusser's account of interpellation, underlying both of which is her appropriation of Derrida's account of the failure of the performative (as previously discussed in Chapters 2 and 3).[2] The main point of the discussion here is that language may be performative, and there may be a sense in which we are injured by language, but that is not to concede that hate speech has the performative power attributed to it by those who draw on speech act theory in the 'hate speech' debates.

Some of the most significant themes that run throughout Butler's work are thus elaborated in *Excitable Speech*. These include: the attempt to theorize the role of language in the production of subjectivity; the implications of this for a theory of agency, which is now referred to as 'discursive' or 'linguistic agency'; the reworking of speech act theory and Althusser's account of interpellation; the ambivalence at the heart of performativity; and the politics of the performative. Alongside this, the analysis of the workings of racist hate speech demonstrates some of the significance of Butler's account of performativity for understanding racial identity and categorization. From the perspective of performativity, this becomes a product of a process of racialization which also involves the iteration and reiteration of speech acts, and which is conceived as an intrinsic aspect of the process of coming into being as an intelligible, embodied subject (subjectification). Developing the theory of performativity in this context thus makes a significant contribution to critical race theory, which also challenges the apparent naturalness of racial categories and seeks to expose the operations of power in their construction. Additionally, Butler's analysis of pornography as hate speech in the arguments of Catherine MacKinnon contributes to debates within feminism about the negative effects pornography has on women, and the extent to which these should be addressed though censorship – if at all. Butler rejects MacKinnon's view of pornography as a form of hate speech which subordinates and silences women and, as such, should be banned. Instead Butler highlights the problems with this view and with state-imposed censorship campaigns. She argues that the latter tend to serve the interests of reactionary political groups rather than to further feminist political goals, and are more often used against gay and lesbian groups than mainstream pornographers and abusers of women and children. Indeed, in examining the relationship between speech and action as it is conceived in the hate speech debates, Butler highlights the performative nature of political discourse itself and the reactionary political interests that often influence state interventions.

Linguistic vulnerability

Excitable Speech begins with a discussion of 'linguistic vulnerability' and what it might mean to claim that we have been injured by language. Butler asks:

> Could language injure us if we were not, in some sense, linguistic beings, beings who require language in order to be? Is our vulnerability to language a consequence of our being constituted within its terms? If we are formed in language, then that formative power precedes and conditions any decision we might make about it, insulting us from the start, as it were, by its prior power.
>
> (Butler 1997a: 1–2)

Furthermore, she also asks, referring to Althusser's notion of interpellation in which 'being called a name is one of the conditions by which a subject is constituted in language' (p. 2): 'Does the power of language to injure follow from its interpellative power? And how, if at all, does linguistic agency emerge from this scene of enabling vulnerability?' (p. 2).

In order to answer these questions, she expands on what it might mean to claim that subjects are 'constituted in discourse' by reassessing the ways in which interpellation, rethought as speech acts, works. This involves rejecting the view that 'the effects of a speech act are necessarily tied to the speech act, its originating or enduring context or indeed its animating intentions or original deployments' (p. 14). It also involves rejecting the view that the injurious effects of speech acts are the product only of spoken works as 'linguistic injury appears to be the effect not only of the words by which one is addressed, but the mode of address itself, a mode – a disposition or bearing – that interpellates and constitutes a subject' (p. 2). At the same time, it involves highlighting 'the open temporality of the speech act' (p. 15) and the gap between speech and action, which produce the possibility for 'counter speech as a kind of talking back' (p. 15). She argues that this provides the possibility for 'linguistic agency as an alternative to the relentless search for legal remedy' (p. 15) in the hate speech campaigns.

In Butler's reformulation of interpellation, she sets Austin's distinction between illocutionary and perlocutionary speech acts in the context of Althusser's account of the role of the 'sovereign voice'. This move allows her to provide a more nuanced account of the workings of speech acts in the constitution of subjectivity, whilst at the same time emphasizing the gap between speech and action that is a significant aspect of her critique of hate speech legislation. This gap is also crucial to the political aspirations of her own project, as it is this that allows for the possibility of change and resignification.

It is also this gap that is the source of her critique of Austin's distinction between illocutionary and perlocutionary speech acts. In the former the effects are immediate, the saying is the doing (e.g. a judge saying 'I condemn you', a registrar saying 'I pronounce you husband and wife'). In the latter they are consequential, that is the effects follow on from the speech act but do not coincide with it. In Austin's account, the force of the speech act (i.e. that which determines that it is effective) lies in the rituals and conventions that bestow authority on the speaker at the time of utterance (the judge in the legal system, the registrar in civil ceremonies); and this can be established by locating the speech act within a 'total speech situation' (p. 3). However, Butler takes issue with this view. She argues that even in the case of illocutionary speech acts, the effectivity of the utterance cannot be contained in that one moment as it too involves a historicity and a futurity whose consequences can neither be known in advance nor controlled by the speaker. Moreover, it is simply not possible to determine a 'total speech situation'. Thus, she says of illocutionary speech acts:

> As utterances, they work to the extent that they are given in

the form of a ritual, that is, repeated in time, and, hence, maintain a sphere of operation that is not restricted to the moment of utterance itself. The illocutionary speech act performs its deed *at the moment of utterance*, and yet to the extent that the moment is ritualized, it is never merely a single moment. The 'moment' in ritual is a condensed historicity: it exceeds itself in past and future directions, an effect of prior and future invocations that constitute and escape the instance of utterance.

(p. 3, original emphasis)

In this sense, the force of the speech act cannot be fixed in the authority or intentions of the speaker. The performativity of speech acts is never as immediate as Austin suggests, as there is always a gap between speech and action.

Butler makes a similar critique of Althusser's account of interpellation as emanating from a sort of divine voice that brings into being that which it names. In an attempt to explain the role of ideology in the constitution of subjectivity through interpellation, Althusser draws an analogy between ideology and a divine voice that names. Butler rejects this analogy. She says: 'The voice is implicated in a notion of sovereign power, power figured as emanating from a subject, activated in a voice, whose effects appear to be the magical effects of that voice' (p. 32). She suggests that the power of the address in acts of interpellation is better read in a more Foucauldian way. Then it can be seen that the force of interpellations, the power which animates them, stems from the citationality, conventionality and historicity of speech acts – 'the force of reiterated convention' (p. 33) – rather than the sovereign voice at the time of utterance. This also better allows for the possibility that the discourses that inaugurate the subject need not take the form of a voice at all but could involve a mode of address that does not use words. Hence: 'Interpellation must be dissociated from the figure of the voice in order to become the instrument and mechanism of discourses whose efficacy is irreducible to their moment of enunciation' (p. 32).

In the case of Althusser's example of the policeman calling to the pedestrian who, in turning round to answer the call, recognizes himself as a pedestrian, the interpellation thus works 'in part through the citational dimension of the speech act, the historicity of convention that exceeds and enables the moment of its enunciation' (p. 33).[3] Indeed, she argues, *contra* Althusser, that the subject does not need to recognize themselves or to turn around to be constituted as a subject: 'For the measure of that constitution is not to be found in a reflexive appropriation of that constitution, but, rather, in a chain of signification that exceeds the circuit of self-knowledge' (p. 33). Furthermore, she goes on: 'The time of discourse is not the time of the subject' (p. 3). In other words, it is not a kind of sovereign power as in the voice which names that makes any particular naming effective because the power of that naming subject is derivative of the 'the force of reiterated convention' (p. 33).

It might help to think of another example here. Consider the pronouncement at birth of 'it's a girl', which Butler herself has used at times to demonstrate the way that performativity works. This starts off the chain of citations that constitute the 'girling' of a girl in her account. However, whilst this may indeed be the case, a girl may not recognize herself in those girling interpellations, even though they are the site of her speaking position. Moreover, these citations may constitute the mode of address through which the girl comes into being but she may also resist them by reciting them in ways that differ from accepted norms – and this resistance need not be intentional. These possibilities arise precisely because the force of the meaning of the utterance 'it's a girl' does not depend on the power of the speaker to name, or even on the anatomy of the infant in question, but on the conventions that are cited in the naming. Becoming a girl thus involves an on-going process of citation and recitation which is the source of what Butler describes as both 'linguistic vulnerability' and 'discursive agency'. This is because, on the one hand, the extent to which a girl deviates from the chain of citations that constitute her as a girl mirrors the extent to which she is recognized as intelligible (or not), and so presents a threat to her linguistic survival. On the other hand, the fact that these citations must be re-cited means that interpellations are never fixed and final and there is always the possibility of resistance to disempowering gender norms.

So what does all this mean in relation to hate speech? Well, it means that there is a fundamental way in which we are all produced in language in a position of subordination, because our social existence is dependent on the address of the other and on being recognizable. So any kind of radical autonomy is just not possible. In that sense we are both already injured and open to further injury. Nevertheless, it does not follow from this that hate speech is necessarily effective. Although we need interpellations to come into being, any particular interpellation *carries within it the possibility to 'restage' it*, to alter its meaning against conventional regulatory norms. So whilst it is through the performativity of discourse – made up of various speech acts as interpellations – that we are constituted as subjects, the particular meanings involved in those speech acts are historical and variable. Hate speech is thus socially contingent and avoidable. It does not work by analogy with a physical injury, as sometimes seems to be implied, for example, when racist speech is described as being like 'a slap in the face' (p. 4) or, as Butler suggests, Delgado and Matsuda seem to be saying in the phrase 'words that wound'. Indeed, this argument relies on an illocutionary model, as if the deed in itself constitutes the injury (rather than the force of reiterated conventions) and there is no gap between words and action. Hence: 'Hate speech exposes a prior vulnerability to language, one that we have by being interpellated kinds of beings, dependent on the address of the other in order to be' (p. 26). However, it doesn't follow from this that hate speech itself exerts an illocutionary performative force and thus has the power to do what it says, in the saying (e.g. because it constitutes you as subordinate you are subordinated).

Moreover, although the perpetrators of hate speech are responsible for their own speech acts, they are not usually the originators of the sentiments these convey. For example: 'Racist speech works through the invocation of convention; it circulates, and though it requires the subject for its speaking, it neither begins nor ends with the subject who speaks or with the specific name that is used' (p. 34). Furthermore, encoded in those conventions is an injurious force that works through 'an encoded memory or a trauma, one that lives in language and is carried in language' (p. 36). Racist hate speech thus involves a kind of historicity, and its force depends on 'a form of repetition that is linked to trauma, on what is, strictly speaking, not remembered, but relived, and relived in and through the linguistic substitution for the traumatic event' (p. 36). This has enormous implications for what to do about hate speech, in all its various forms. Not least in the sense that, if the hate speech in question gains its force from established meanings and pre-existing contexts, censoring particular speech acts will not make those contexts disappear. Furthermore, not only is the argument that hate speech exerts an illocutionary force theoretically flawed, in Butler's view, but to argue that it does so would be to foreclose a critical response and so neglect the possibility of 'discursive agency', which is the source of Butler's political optimism.

Discursive agency

The crucial political point of her arguments in *Excitable Speech* is captured in Butler's remark in the introduction:

> I wish to question for the moment the presumption that hate speech always works, not to minimize the pain that is suffered as a consequence of hate speech, but to leave open the possibility that its failure is the condition of a critical response.
>
> (Butler 1997a: 19)

She goes on: 'If the account of the injury of hate speech forecloses the possibility of a critical response to that injury, the account confirms the totalizing effects of such an injury' (p. 19). It is thus the apparent success of hate speech as a constituting power in the work of legal scholars and philosophers, such as MacKinnon, Langton and Matsuda, that Butler's analysis seeks to challenge. She wants to focus instead on the 'fault lines' that inhibit the success of hate speech and that might lead 'to the undoing of this process of discursive constitution' (p. 19). It is the open-endedness and temporality of speech acts in her account of linguistic vulnerability and discursive agency that provide this. This is due to the need for constant citation and recitation, and the impossibility of fixing the effects of those acts in either the moment of utterance or the authority and intentions of the speaker.

For example, Butler argues that Matsuda's account of hate speech

> presumes that a social structure is enunciated at the moment of the hateful utterance; hate speech reinvokes the position of dominance, and reconsolidates it at the moment of utterance. As the linguistic rearticulation of social domination, hate speech becomes, for Matsuda, the site for the mechanical and predictable reproduction of power.
>
> (p. 19)

Butler, however, suggests that this view of hate speech does not take into account the temporal aspect of speech acts; that they are subject to iteration and rearticulation. Thus she asks:

> Might the speech act of hate speech be understood as less efficacious, more prone to innovation and subversion, if we take into account the temporal life of the 'structure' it is said to enunciate? If such a structure is dependent upon its enunciation for its continuation, then it is at the site of enunciation that the question of its continuity is to be posed.
>
> (p. 19)

And she goes on:

> Can there be an enunciation that discontinues that structure, or one that subverts that structure through its repetition in speech? As an invocation, hate speech is an act that recalls prior acts, requiring a future repetition to endure. Is there a repetition that might disjoin the speech act from its supporting conventions such that its repetition confounds rather than consolidates its injurious efficacy?
>
> (pp. 19–20)

This is possible if the performativity of speech acts is understood, as Butler argues in *Excitable Speech*, with Derrida and *contra* Austin, as both defined by the social context in which they take place yet always capable of breaking with that context. This involves emphasizing the 'ambivalent structure at the heart of performativity' which Butler has insisted on throughout her work. Speech acts do not simply reflect social power, established social conditions or official discourse but, rather, always involve the possibility of subversive resignification.[4]

Theoretically, then, this understanding of the workings of speech acts illuminates the relationship between language and the social and provides a way of understanding the inter-implication of the two. In particular, it provides a theory of language and signification, which highlights the problems with understanding the performativity of speech acts as merely reflecting the social rather than themselves producing social effects. Social effects, moreover, which are not always predictable, and which are never entirely in the control of the speaker. Butler's analyses of hate speech regulation attempts to demonstrate this, as well as the pitfalls of relying on legal remedies.

Racist hate speech

In 'Burning Acts, Injurious Speech' Butler discusses the United States Supreme Court's decision that a white teenager burning a cross outside the home of a black family should be construed as a form of speech, protected by the First Amendment rather than threatening conduct or 'fighting words' from which the family in question should be protected. This is compared to another case in which the same court decided that racist speech was acceptable as evidence that a crime could be racially motivated. Significantly however, the charge in this latter case was against some young black men who attacked a young white man after watching the film *Mississippi Burning*. This film portrays the racism of the Klu Klux Klan and the apparent failures of the legal system to deal with this. It depicts the murder of civil rights campaigners by the Klansmen and the use of burning crosses and firebombs to threaten people who are seen to help the Justice Department.

Butler highlights the ambiguities involved in the decisions in each of these cases. Her analysis also reveals the way in which the attribution of speech or conduct to forms of hate speech is apparently open to manipulation. Furthermore, she argues that such decisions by the judiciary amount to a form of injurious speech themselves. Hence:

I want to suggest that the court's speech carries with it its own violence, and that the very institution that is invested with the authority to adjudicate the problem of hate speech recirculates and redirects that hatred in and as its own highly consequential speech, often by coopting the very language that it seeks to adjudicate.

(Butler 1997a: 54)

Butler reports that in the case of the burning cross, the judge's reasoning involved the view that although it was 'reprehensible,' it was nevertheless not a case of fighting words but the articulation of a viewpoint, and therefore must be protected as the expression of free speech. Furthermore, it was also stated that it was 'unconstitutional to impose prohibitions on speech solely on the basis of the "content" or "subjects addressed" in that speech' (p. 53). This effectively removes the significance of the whiteness of the cross burner and the blackness of the family from the reasoning in the justice's decision. The history of violence against black people and civil rights workers that the burning cross symbolizes and the threat it conveys were thus not able to be taken into account.[5]

Moreover, Butler's examination of the wording of the arguments on which the court's decision was based suggests that there seems to be a shift from 'the need for protection from racist speech to the need for protection from public protest against racism' (p. 57). Indeed, her careful 'rhetorical' analysis of the reasoning of the judges results in the view that

the question of whether or not the black family in Minnesota is entitled to protection from public displays such as cross-burnings is displaced onto the question of whether or not the 'content' of free speech is to be protected from those who would burn it. The fire is thus displaced from the cross to the legal instrument wielded by those who would protect the black family from the fire, but then to the black family itself, to blackness, to the vacant lot, to rioters in Los Angeles who explicitly oppose the decision of a court and who now represent the incendiary power of the traumatized rage of black people who would burn the judiciary itself.

(p. 59)[6]

Butler thus aims to show how the initial threat that the burning cross presented to the black family is reconceived, in the rhetoric of the judge's decision, as a fire that threatens to incinerate the First Amendment and 'spark' an uprising against the judiciary. The threat with which they are dealing somehow becomes a threat to the legal system itself. 'Thus the court protects the burning cross as free speech, figuring those it injures as the true threat, elevating the burning cross as a deputy for the court, the local protector and token of free speech' (p. 65).

Butler's analysis thus highlights a kind of violence involved in the court's decision which, in effect performs its own injurious speech, and appears to support racist 'actions' rather than protect the victims of racist intimidation from the threat of racist violence. It emphasizes the limitations of state interventions to protect against hate speech and demonstrates the way in which hate speech legislation can be used to further conservative agendas – in this case racism, in others sexism and homophobia – and to impede progressive aims, because the courts have the power to decide what will and what won't count as hate speech. The court's decisions in these two cases did little to undermine the racist rituals, which the racist hate speech reiterated. Indeed, the opposite would appear to be the case, as the decisions in these cases, seemed rather to reiterate those racist rituals too.

Hate speech and pornography

Butler also finds the use of speech act theory in feminist campaigns against pornography more problematic than helpful. Indeed, there has been extensive debate within feminism about the negative effects pornography has on women, including the extent to which it constructs women as subordinate, and the ways in which it contributes to violence against women and children; and there continues to be little agreement about the extent to which legal regulation is required to combat this. The debates range from anti-pornography campaigners who, broadly speaking, argue that pornography contributes to the widespread trafficking in women and children and the institution of sexual slavery and so should be banned; to feminists who campaign against censorship who, broadly speaking, argue that it would not (and does not) protect women and children from these practices and that they would be better served by bringing pornography into the open, along with its production and distribution. However, this apparent polarization somewhat simplifies the complexity of feminist perspectives in these debates; moreover, Butler's analysis of pornography as hate speech in the work of Catherine MacKinnon does not involve an explicit engagement with them. Nevertheless, there is a sense in which her arguments in *Excitable Speech* highlight the limitations of anti-pornography arguments and instead lend support to those of feminists who argue against censorship.[7]

In *Only Words*, MacKinnon (1993) employs speech act theory to argue that pornography is hate speech and, as such, exerts a performative force that is not just *perlocutionary* (which would mean that it has harmful consequences), but *illocutionary*, as it constitutes women as a group or class as subordinate. As such, it effectively silences women by depriving them of a speaking position except in pornographic terms. Indeed, MacKinnon argues that pornographic representation constitutes an injurious act against women in the same sort of sense that the burning cross outside the home of a black family constitutes an act of discrimination. However, Butler argues against this analogy as: 'The theory of representation and, indeed, the theory of performativity at work differs in each of these cases' (p. 21). She goes on to argue that this analogy 'is not only a mistake in judgement, but the exploitation of the sign of racial violence for the purposes of enhancing, through a metonymical slippage, the putatively injurious power of pornography' (p. 21). Moreover, Butler is concerned about the ways in which the increased potential for state intervention in relation to explicit sexual material presents a threat to lesbian and gay politics. These often depend on the publication of such material. She gives the examples of 'graphic self-representation', for example, Mapplethorpe's photography;[8] 'explicit self-declaration', for example coming out as gay or lesbian; and 'explicit sexual education', as in relation to AIDS, which have all been construed by conservative critics as speech acts which amount to injurious conduct.

Butler is also concerned with MacKinnon's assumption that pornography has the power to act as an 'imperative, and that this imperative has the power to realize that which it dictates'

(p. 65). In MacKinnon's argument, it would seem that is not just that pornographic images of women enact a range of misogynistic fantasies, or even that they give expression to misogynistic social structures; it is rather that they construct a pornographic *reality*.

The hate speech of pornography as an institution is construed as having the power to do that. It is not just the speech acts of individual pornographers that are in question in MacKinnon's view of pornography as hate speech; it is the injurious conduct of pornographic representation or visual imagery that is alleged to act in this way.

Hence Butler cites MacKinnon at length, including:

> Pornography makes the world a pornographic place through its making and use, establishing what women are said to exist as, are seen as, are treated as, constructing the social reality of what a woman is and can be in terms of what can be done to her, and what a man is in terms of doing it.
> (MacKinnon 1993: 25, cited in Butler 1997a: 66)

Butler, however, rejects the view that pornographic images have the power to work in this way to construct a pornographic reality. She argues that MacKinnon's argument involves transposing the visual field of pornographic images into a speaking subject with 'the power to bring into being that which it names, to wield an efficacious power analogous to the divine performative' (p. 66). Thus, visual images are not only transformed into a linguistic field, they are accorded an unwarranted felicity as well. It is as if the images that command an act of sexual subordination in so doing performatively produce the social reality of women as subordinate – and silenced – by encoding 'the will of masculine authority, and compelling a compliance with its command' (p. 67). For Butler, however, this is a dubious source of authority based on an unwarranted leap from what is done in the *depiction* of pornography to the suggestion that this is what pornography itself does, as if the depiction in pornography is realized and so constitutes reality for women as a group. In MacKinnon's argument, representation becomes reality; pornography is construed as both speech and conduct, and the gap between speech and conduct is eclipsed.

Against this view, Butler argues that the imperative that MacKinnon describes in the pornographic depiction fails to deliver in reality. The visual field does not work as an efficacious speech act because 'the performativity of a text is not under sovereign control' (p. 69) as her critique of Austin's and Althusser's account of the workings of speech acts demonstrates. Hence, pornography may well be offensive but it does not have the power to act in a performative way to produce in reality that which is depicted in visual images. Instead, she argues, the power of pornographic images is better understood as stemming from the depiction of 'hyperbolic' gender norms, and unrealizable positions that 'hold sway' over the social reality of gender positions, but do not actually constitute that reality. Indeed, this very unreality is both 'its condition and its lure' (p. 69). Pornographic representation thus represents *imaginary* relations that both re-enact and exaggerate gender norms. Rather than representing what women *are*, as MacKinnon suggests, pornographic images of women's subordination present an allegorical account of 'masculine will and feminine submission' (p. 69). Censoring those images would not rid the world of those 'insistent and faulty imaginary relations' or the misogyny they depict. The task for feminist criticism is therefore not to seek to abolish pornography but to read such texts against the grain and resist the kind of literalization involved in MacKinnon's arguments; and, once again, to consider 'the possibility of resignification as an alternative reading of performativity and politics' (p. 69).

To sum up then, the main differences between Butler's account of speech act theory and those involved in the hate speech debates in the US stem from Butler's insistence that, although we are in some sense linguistically constituted, it does not necessarily follow from this that we are linguistically determined, either by the performative force of racist hate speech or pornographic representations conceived as hate speech or, indeed, any other forms of hate speech. This is because of the excitability and temporality of speech acts, which renders them out of control and unpredictable, as well as open-ended and citational, and thus continually in need of iteration and reiteration. It might be through speech acts that we come into being, because they confer social existence, but those speech acts must be repeated and, since that repetition is not merely mechanical, this always involves the possibility of appropriation and reiteration in unintended ways. Hence, despite Butler's own emphasis on the performativity of 'speech', she nevertheless resists the move to conflate speech with conduct on which hate speech legislation depends. This would be to succumb to the 'the fantasy of sovereign power in speech' which underpins the work of Austin and Althusser. Butler argues that the injurious aspects of hate speech cannot be fixed in the speech act itself, or the intentions or authority of the speaker, as this fantasy suggests. This is because of the gap (or incommensurability) between saying and meaning, which stems from the inherent repeatability of speech acts, and that the force of reiterated conventions depends on that inherent repeatability.

So, although Butler is not against 'any and all regulation', in her view 'the ritual chain of hateful speech cannot be effectively countered by means of censorship' (p. 102). Since hate speech involves citing and reciting meanings that are already established as hateful, and that get their force from that historicity, 'the question will be whether the state or public discourse take up that practice of reneactment' (p. 102). That her account of the workings of speech acts does not provide a means to predict whether they will or not is perhaps the greatest limitation of this approach for those who wish to effect concrete political change, and a source of some criticism to this effect.

Political implications and social change

It is clear then that the series of analyses in *Excitable Speech* serve to further Butler's theoretical project in relation to the workings of speech acts in the constitution of subjectivity, and the possibility of linguistic agency. However, although this has far-reaching political implications, it does not in itself provide a 'set of clarifying solutions to the contemporary operation of the speech act' (p. 20), as Butler herself is well aware. It does the important work of identifying the potentially injurious speech of the state in the operations of hate speech legislation and identifying the racism, misogyny and conservative agendas that often implicitly structure legal decisions. And it provides the *possibility* for the change and transformation of the frameworks of meaning that structure the regulatory norms (i.e. the social regulation and constitutive constraints) through which we come into being and exert any agency at all – through the possibility of linguistic or discursive agency. However, one criticism of these developments is not just that her account does not specify a concrete programme for social change, though this criticism continues to be made in relation to the moves in *Excitable Speech*. More than that, it is claimed that the theoretical approach involved undermines the very possibility of the expressed political aims because this account of the workings of hate speech forecloses the possibility of 'real change' (Schaff 2002).

Schaff argues that the focus on resignification as a political strategy amounts to a form of 'self-serving libertarianism' and an abuse of Foucault's account of power because it individual- izes the possibility for change. In fact, she suggests that this strategy parallels traditional liberal theory in which an appeal to individual agency masks group-based oppression (Schaff 2002: 196). However, Butler's account of agency highlights the work- ings of power in ways that go unrecognized in traditional liberal theory, and precisely because of this, it helps to identify rather than mask group-based forms of oppression, as her analysis of hate speech demonstrates in relation to racism and homosexuals in the military.[9] Moreover, unlike traditional notions of agency, discursive or linguistic agency is not a property of individuals. The force of its operations lies in the potential it brings for change and transformation on a wider level than that of the individual, in the implicit power relations that structure the lives and social relations of oppressed groups through the operations of discourses and chains of signification in the constitution of subjectivity.

Furthermore, rather than amounting to a misappropriation of Foucault's account of power, as Schaff suggests, it could be argued that Butler's emphasis on the role of resignification and the redeployment of conventional norms in challenging the regulatory frameworks (and speech acts) that 'discipline' us, furthers his work. In particular, it could be seen as contri- buting to the issues and debates of 'What is Enlightenment?' (Foucault 1984) as well furthering the attempt to develop a critical ontology of the present, including ourselves, in his genealogies. Indeed, there is a sense in which Butler's analysis of hate speech can be seen as furthering Foucault's endeavours by unmasking the ways in which particular meanings come to be possible in relation to sex, gender and identity by revealing certain 'subjugated knowledges' and the implicit workings of racist and hetero-normative power relations. Alongside this, Butler's wider project clearly contributes to challenging hetero-normative power relations and producing new forms of knowledge about the nature of ontology and the workings of discourse, or discursive fields, in the constitution of subjectivity and the body. Indeed, hate speech could be seen as operating in various discursive fields.

Furthermore, Schaff highlights the limitations of employing counter-speech as a strategy in practical terms, by pointing out that reclaiming the language of 'queer' does not protect individual gay people from physical attack from homophobic gangs. The point though is that the state censoring of hate speech does not afford this kind of protection either. Indeed, gay individuals already have the protection of the law from physical assault from homophobic gangs, in theory at least, but this does not prevent all forms of 'gay bashing'. (It did not prevent the deaths of Venus Xtravaganza or Teena Brandon, discussed in Chapter 5.) Indeed, as Butler's analysis of hate speech regulation by the courts suggests, such legislation might not afford as much protection to the victims of hate speech as those who argue for state censorship might assume. Nor is Butler arguing against any form of legislation so much as highlighting the limits and risks that state intervention entails.

Indeed, Schaff's criticisms of Butler's account of hate speech are a bit like those criticisms of Foucault that claim that his account of power as insidious, relational and capillary ignores structural features and the state, which miss the point that his view of power does not involve dismissing the state as wielding any form of power. It is rather a means of recognizing that the exercise of state power should not be the starting point for an analysis of the workings of power in contemporary societies. Furthermore, if this is the case, it is hardly surprising that state power cannot provide the answer to the operations of hate speech, and may indeed itself actively contribute to it, precisely because of the implicit operations of power (and signification) that structure court decisions, as Butler's analysis has shown.

To return to the question of whether Butler's account of the workings of hate speech enables the possibility of 'real change' then; and, relatedly, the issue of whether counter-speech amounts to an effective strategy against prevailing forms of power. The answer to these questions clearly lies in the perception of 'real' change, and the understanding of the ways in which prevailing forms of power work. The 'real' change with which Butler's politics of the performative is concerned is change at the level of the meanings that shape the possibilities for hate speech to exist in the form it does, as well as for it to exist at all – though not in a Habermasian sense.[10] From this perspective it is only by effecting change in the possibility of meanings that any 'real' changes will occur. Legal remedies such as censorship can address only particular instances, not the general field of meanings that brought into being those possibilities in the first place. To return to the example of racist hate speech that Butler discusses: racist hate speech exists and can work only because of the chain of signification, which involves the citation and recitation of conventional meanings. The burning cross was effective as a threat to the black family because of its associations with white supremacists, and the history of lynching and arson attacks on the property of black people, and others who sympathized with their claims for civil rights, by Klansmen. The court that decided the case in Butler's analysis could not see that the chain of signification through which the judges read this speech act incorporated an implicit racism which constructs black bodies as threatening. Hate speech legislation did not help the black family or protect them from linguistic harm. Quite the opposite, as it seemed to support the racist act as the expression of a valid viewpoint, which overrode the ways in which that expression caused harm to those to whom it was addressed. In this sense the hate speech legislation had the effect of operating its own form of violence against that family, as Butler argues. What needs to be changed then, to undermine the force of such acts, are the frameworks of meaning, the chain of signification, that produces black people themselves as a threat; to cite and recite the meaning of 'blackness' or 'African American' in non-conventional, more positive ways. The history of racism that gave rise to the burning of crosses as a threat against black people and their property cannot be changed, but how it is understood and represented – what it means – is open to change and expropriation. This is the sense in which counter-speech can work as a strategy against prevailing forms of power. Without it, censoring individual speech acts is unlikely to make much difference.

5   Beyond identity politics
Gender, transgender and sexual difference

Butler's account of performativity and critique of identity categories has had significant implications for feminist and queer politics, as we have seen. It involves a shift from identity politics, based on sameness and the policing of boundaries, to a politics of identification which involves the continual examination of the (political) construction of identities, and careful attention to the exclusions on which any identities are based. This move to a politics of identity in Butler's work involves a shift in the understanding of resistance and change that is similar to that which characterizes Foucault's work. This could be described as a shift from a concern with freedom and liberation, in an Enlightenment or modernist sense, to an emphasis on resistance and struggle. Just as this shift in Foucault's work has been found to be liberating to some, and politically debilitating to others, so it is with Butler's work. Foucault's account has been criticized as politically debilitating if freedom and liberation, rooted in universal truth, are no longer to be perceived as the goals of political action. Similarly, Butler's account of performativity is criticized as politically debilitating if there is no independently existing body on which to base our feminist and queer projects and no independent truths of sex, gender and sexuality on which we can build our identity, including trans identity, not even the duality of sexual difference.

Whilst some of these issues have been discussed in earlier chapters, especially Chapter 2 in relation to feminist projects and the materiality of the body, this chapter examines the significance of Butler's account of performativity and politics of identity for trans theories and politics; and the significance of

transgender and transsexuality for Butler's account of performativity, and the understanding of resistance and change it
involves. In particular, it examines the significance of Butler's
account of the performativity of the body for trans theories that
insist on the significance of the materiality of the trans body 'as
telos' (Prosser 1998: 33); and it examines the significance of
trans identity for Butler's critique of sexual difference in an
essential binary form. The implications of trans experience for
theorizing the relationship between sex, gender and the body in
terms of 'body image' is also considered in the context of Butler's
account of performativity. It is argued that trans[1] experiences,
when examined in this way, would seem to undermine the
givenness of sexual difference that underpins feminist theories
of the imaginary body.

Indeed, there has been much debate within feminism and queer
theory about the political possibilities of transgender and transsexuality and the subversive potential of trans identity and
politics. A significant issue in these debates concerns whether the
refusal of the connection between sex and gender, biology and
gender identity, undermines and transcends the binary system of
sex and gender. Or whether it is rather that sex reassignment
surgery, which involves changing the body to match a person's
gender identity, indicates capitulation to it. Furthermore, whilst
gender ambiguities, cross-dressing and other forms of politically
strategic transgendering are seen as one step on the road towards
ridding the world of 'gender oppression' by those who advocate
it, for many trans individuals, the goal is not so much to rid the
world of gender oppression as to find a space for themselves in
which their gender identity matches the sex of their biological
body. The aim is not to stand out and transgress, but to fit in and
belong, to be 'normal'. Trans sex in this sense becomes a matter
of assimilation rather than resistance and, far from undermining
the binary system of sex and gender, would seem to reinforce it.

This tension results in some very different political goals for
trans activists. Roen, for example, contrasts the differing political goals of a 'radical politics of gender transgression' and a
'liberal transsexual politics' (Roen 2001: 503). Although there is
some overlap between these groups, not least in that they both
seek greater acceptance of trans people, a significant difference
is that the radical politics of gender transgression wants more

acceptance for gender ambiguity. The aim here is transgression and opening up the boundaries of sex/gender. In contrast to this, the aims of a liberal transsexual politics are to make living as the 'the other sex', that is the sex that the trans person feels him or herself to be, more acceptable. This may involve the view that sex reassignment surgery results not in transsexuality, but in passing as a woman or man, and the political goal is equal rights for transsexuals so that they have the possibility to do so.

When these tensions are set in the context of Butler's account of performativity, it seems that there are significant limitations to the political goal of trying to establish trans identities as subject positions in their own right that is at the heart of some queer theory and activism.[2] Although there is much to be said for such 'queer' visibility, from the perspective of Butler's account of performativity, making sense of trans experiences requires more than establishing trans identities as subject positions in their own right. One reason for this is that such subject positions still take the binary as the starting point of their identities, one way or another, even as they transgress it (not least those that involve realigning the physical body to match the perceived gender identity) and thus the full force of the challenge to heterosexist sexual difference is undermined. Hence, trans subject positions are likely to remain marginalized as exceptions that prove the rule in the dominant binary framework. What is required therefore is the rearticulation of that binary framework.

In order to demonstrate this, the goals of trans individuals whose aim is to 'pass' and belong are considered in the context of Butler's account of the performativity of the body. Despite the various critiques of Butler's own treatment of transsexuality/transgender in *Gender Trouble* and in her analysis of *Paris is Burning* (Namaste 1996; Prosser 1998), it is argued that her account of performativity provides a view of the materiality of the body, and critique of the duality of sexual difference, as a product of construction that is in keeping with transsexuals' own accounts of the experiences of being in the 'wrong' body.[3] This is not, however, in the sense of providing a metaphor for the fluidity of gender and sexuality, as some postmodern accounts might want to suggest. Indeed, to reiterate an earlier point, it is not that Butler's account of performativity provides a way of explaining the *fluidity* of gender and sexuality. It is more that it provides an account of the *intractability* of identity categories and a way of understanding their role in the materialization of the body, whilst at the same time revealing their roots in social and political regulation rather than anatomy or nature.[4] It is this intractability and understanding of materialization that are most useful when considering trans experiences of the 'wrong' body. However, it is also Butler's refusal to accord the body any role in the materialization of the body (or body narratives) that has come under most criticism from trans perspectives. This criticism is examined in the work of Jay Prosser (1998).

These tensions are also reflected in the different views within feminism on the significance and status of male-to-female (mtf) transsexuals. Mtf transsexuals have encountered hostility from some quarters because they transcend gender categories, and from others because they reaffirm them (More 1999), sometimes in overly stereotypical ways. Indeed, there has been some reluctance amongst feminists to accept such people as women. However, when these tensions are set in the context of Butler's account of performativity, it would seem that feminist theory has much to gain from the insights that trans experiences bring to feminists' attempts to theorize the relationship between sex, gender, sexuality and the body, especially in relation to the apparent givenness and significance of sexual difference.

In order to demonstrate this, the implications of trans experience for theorizing the relationship between sex, gender and the body in theories of 'body image' are considered in this chapter, focusing on the work of Elizabeth Grosz and Moira Gatens. Their work involves combining a more phenomenological approach that focuses on the 'lived body', with psychoanalytic insights concerning the mediated nature of bodily experiences, to develop the concept of 'the imaginary body'.[5] The aim is to give the body a more prominent role in the production of gendered subjectivities than Butler's account would seem to allow, whilst continuing to avoid any kind of biological or psychological reductionism. However, it is argued that trans experiences would seem to undermine the givenness of sexual difference that underpins these accounts of imaginary bodies. From the perspective of performativity, trans experiences can be seen as ways of doing gender and sexuality beyond the binary frame, even in those cases which seem ultimately to capitulate to it.

Hence, it is argued that they contribute to the 'remapping of sexual difference itself' and displacing what Butler describes as the 'hegemonic symbolic of (heterosexist) sexual difference' (Butler 1993a: 91).

However, the 'remapping of sexual difference' is one thing, and displacing the hegemonic symbolic is another. The latter requires the former but this doesn't guarantee it.

Butler on performativity and materiality

That this remapping of sexual difference is possible, as well as necessary, in Butler's account of performativity, is due to Butler's formulation of sexual difference as a normative constraint through which bodies come into being in the process of their materialization. This allows her to focus on the way that the category of sex, and thus sexual difference, is not immutable as it is often taken to be in feminist theories, especially those that focus on sexual difference rather than gender (as discussed in Chapter 2). Butler argues that understanding the body as the foundation of these binary categories is a product of regimes of power/knowledge in a Foucauldian sense which have vested interests 'in keeping the body bounded and constituted by markers of sex' (1990a: 129). Hence, she develops her account of the materialization of the body in and through regimes of power/knowledge, such as compulsory heterosexuality and phallogocentrism (and her critique of the binary form of sexual difference which is integral to them) in *Bodies that Matter*.

As well as all this, Butler's account of materialization involves analysing the ways that some bodies are rendered intelligible and some bodies are not. Furthermore, intelligibility also involves the matter of recognition, as she says in an interview with Kate More in 1997 (More 1999), emphasizing her turn to Hegel in *The Psychic Life of Power*, which is a significant but not necessarily always particularly appreciated aspect of her work. Recognition is a concept adapted from Hegel (Butler 1997b) to explain the acquisition of subjectivity as a product of social regulation in a way that is nevertheless intrinsic to our being (as discussed in Chapter 3). This combination of Foucault and Hegel, in the context of Althusser's account of interpellation, leads to the view that 'what we are is a function of the discursive categories that are available for recognition' (Butler in More 1999: 287). In this sense those categories are necessary and indispensable, even as they are not also fully determining. And intelligibility and recognition are very significant issues for trans individuals and theorists, whether the aim is to challenge the boundaries of contemporary categorization or to fit into them and belong.

Indeed, the struggle for intelligibility and recognition in the experiences of trans individuals clearly demonstrates both the necessity and the inadequacy of the categories, and that they are not fully determining. The problem for them is that they do not recognize themselves in the (discursive) categories that are given to them (based on their bodily features), and that they are not recognized by others in the categories to which they aspire if they do not succeed in 'passing'. What is required therefore is a rethinking of the categories themselves, including the categories of the body, gender, sexual difference, heterosexuality, homosexuality and desire. And this is what Butler suggests in *Bodies that Matter* and what she attempts to do in her account of performativity. Furthermore one aspect of this rethinking that is suggested in *Bodies that Matter* is to 'inhabit those categories differently', which, it could be argued, is precisely what trans individuals do, including even post-operative transsexuals, whether this is intentional or not. In this sense trans experiences, could be seen as contributing to what Butler describes as 'the remapping of sexual difference'. Furthermore, from the perspective of Butler's account of performativity, it can be seen that whilst rendering trans bodies and identities intelligible involves the need for public recognition and citizenship rights (which are the aims of campaigning groups such as 'Press for Change', accessible at http://www.pfc.org.uk), such moves are unlikely to produce mainstream intelligibility and recognition unless the binary understanding of sexual difference, which is rooted in what she describes as 'compulsory heterosexuality' and 'phallogocentrism', is displaced.

One of the problems in Butler's account of the performativity of sex and gender stems from her insistence that it makes no sense to think of the materiality of the body outside of a process of construction. This is because there is simply no way to get outside of the cultural frameworks (or, to be more precise, language and signification) that articulate experience in order to get at that materiality, or indeed anything essential, anything in and of itself. This refusal to accord bodies any status outside of their cultural articulation is perhaps the biggest stumbling block in Butler's account of performativity for feminists and trans theorists who engage with her work, and the source of much criticism (some of which is discussed in Chapter 2). Butler, however, insists that this refusal is not to imply that bodies are immaterial but rather to emphasise the materiality of significations and regulatory frameworks through which bodies come into being and embodied subjects achieve cultural intelligibility (or not). The aim, to reiterate, is to deconstruct the notions of the body and materiality in order to reveal how they have 'been deployed as instruments of repressive power' (Butler 1993a: 17) and to reveal the category of sex to be a principle of production and regulation rather than simply a representation of a prior materiality.

It could be argued that, despite concerns about a lack of attention to the materiality of the body (which will be examined below), the focus on the cultural constitution of that materiality as sexed, in a process of materialization that is shaped by compulsory heterosexuality and phallogocentrism, would surely serve the interests of trans individuals and theorists in making sense of their bodies, as trans. Not least because their experiences make explicit the suffering that stems from what the trans performance artist Orlan aptly describes as 'oppressive structures of knowing' (cited in Morgan 1999: 234) and their bodily experiences disrupt the regulatory force of the category of sex. Butler's approach involves revealing the instability on which such categories are based, and exposing the violence and exclusion that underpin any apparent coherence. The exclusion of trans identities and trans individuals from viable subject positions in some feminist and psychoanalytic theories, not to mention the hostility of some feminists to mtf, are also surely examples of that violence and exclusion at work.

Although Butler's account of performativity does not involve making the body, in its corporeality or materiality, the source of its materialization, she still insists that this does not involve negating the matter of the body. She argues that it rather involves freeing the body and the concept of matter from metaphysical constraints and opening them up to political scrutiny (which was discussed in Chapter 2). To sum up the earlier discussion here, although Butler's work is not concerned with metaphysical questions of sex, gender and body *per se*, her critique of these categories involves addressing the metaphysical presuppositions that inform dominant understandings of them. She argues that this may involve a loss of epistemological certainty, as any such certainty is illusory, but it could also offer the possibility of 'new ways for bodies to matter' (Butler 1993a: 30). And the possibility of this is of major concern for Butler, just as it is for trans theorists and activists.

However, challenging and disrupting regimes of power knowledge that constitute us as embodied subjects and rethinking the categories of sex and gender as Butler suggests is no simple matter. Her aim, as she puts it in *Gender Trouble*, is to open up the categories of sex, gender, sexuality, identity and the body to multiple determinations and a proliferation of genders and sexes 'to resignify bodies beyond the binary frame'. In *Bodies that Matter* she explains that the task is not simply to multiply subject positions within the existing symbolic (as some trans theorists aim to do) but to attempt the rearticulation of the symbolic itself.

This was explained in Chapter 2 in relation to the difference between Butler's strategies for change and those of sexual difference theorists such as Kristeva and Irigaray. Although these are complex issues, to sum them up briefly for our concerns here: Butler argues that Kristeva's and Irigaray's attempts to establish alternative subject positions for women ultimately conform to the heterosexual imperative by keeping the duality of sexual difference, and the male/female binary, intact. This involves succumbing to the reification of sexual difference as it is constructed in normative heterosexuality which, Butler argues, is foundational to the work of Freud and Lacan, and on which both Kristeva and Irigaray draw. In terms of strategies for change, Butler's aim is rather 'to reconfigure the mapping of sexual difference itself' (Butler 1993a: 91). Hence, she develops her account of performativity through an alternative reading of the insights of psychoanalysis to suggest that change needs to be directed at the level of the morphological imaginary, since it is through this that sexed identifications are produced and bodies are materialized.

Thus Butler's account of performativity involves focusing on the materiality of significations and the regulatory frameworks through which embodied subjects achieve cultural intelligibility, or not. She wants to reveal that these are shaped by a symbolic order that is both phallocentric and heterosexist, and which depends for its stability on the exclusion and repudiation of the abject of heterosex: and trans people could be included in this category. Indeed, Butler herself says that transgender has always been a concern of hers, though not always explicitly, and she regards her work as theoretically sympathetic to trans concerns (More 1999).

The route to change and transformation in Butler's work therefore becomes a matter of disrupting the workings of the heterosexual imperative, which shapes the hegemonic imaginary, by denaturalizing it and reaffirming the abject of heterosex. The aim of this reaffirmation is to bring the culturally unintelligible into the realm of intelligibility. This is the way to produce 'a potentially productive crisis' which will allow the possibility of 'reconfiguring the mapping of sexual difference' and allow the space for the emergence of an alternative, anti-heterosexist imaginary. Trans individuals and theories would benefit from that and can also be seen as contributing to it.

Indeed, Butler's account of performativity has been highly influential amongst queer theorists and transgender theorists (e.g. Whittle 1996, 2002; Halberstam 1998; Prosser 1998; Sullivan 2003). It provides a theoretical framework for making sense of trans experiences, which also seem to give testimony to the constructedness of the body and identity, outside of the binary framework of male and female. The destabilization of identity involved in Butler's account of performativity fits in with the experiences of transsexuals, whose own aims are to promote a politics of destabilization and the disruption of traditional sex and gender categories (e.g. Bornstein 1994; Halberstam 1998; Stone 1991). However, these political aims do not sit well with people whose aim is to fit in and pass as 'normal'. This isn't an argument for allowing people to 'pass' within existing frameworks or for establishing trans identity in its own right, so much as a strategy aimed at enabling someone in what is currently felt to be the 'wrong body' (by themselves and/or by others) to be accepted as the gender that they feel themselves to be, in the right body. For example, Stephen Whittle (2000, 2002), founder of 'Press for Change', provides an account of how he has known himself to be a boy from childhood despite his apparently female body; and how he has struggled to establish the legal status of father to his two children. (Happily, this has now been established following the Gender Recognition Act, 2004, in the UK.) However the problem remains that getting recognition in this way, in the gender that is identified with, involves surgical realignment. Achieving cultural intelligibility involves modifying the body to match the (felt) gender, rather than acceptance of that body and the felt gender as intelligible in themselves. This would require resignifying the categories of sex and gender beyond the binary frame.

Trans critiques

Turning now to the issue of the materiality of the body and trans critiques of Butler's work: refusing to allow the body any role in the process of materialization has been criticized by trans theorists who want to accord the materiality of the lived body some sort of causal role in the experience of sexuality, in particular Prosser (1998). Indeed, Prosser is critical of any attempt to theorize the social constitution of identity without taking account of the role of the body in its corporeality and literality. He insists that it is a mistake to ignore this aspect which he feels transsexuals' accounts of embodiment clearly demonstrate to be significant. Hence he wants to 'to read individual corporeal experience back into theories of "the" body', even though he recognizes some of the difficulties with this and he suggests it needs to be done with 'humbling tentativeness' (Prosser 1998: 7, citing Lynne Segal).

Prosser is also highly critical of the association of transgender and transsexuality with queer in queer theory in general, and in Butler's work in particular. He claims that it was *Gender Trouble* that was mainly responsible for associating transgender with queer sexuality in the first place (Prosser 1998: 24). He is especially critical of the way that transgender and transsexuality are undifferentiated in *Gender Trouble* and, along with butches and drag queens, are used to highlight the performativity of gender and thus the 'inessentiality of sex and nonoriginality of heterosexuality' (p. 26).

Prosser objects to this use of transgender and transsexuality in *Gender Trouble* from the perspective of those individuals whose aim is to pass. There are three main reasons for his objections to this that can usefully be considered here. The first stems from the desire for assimilation as 'real' women or men, and the desire to 'belong' in the body narratives of transsexuals; as well as the fact that not all transsexuals are queer, either in the sense of homosexual or, even (alluding to Butler's work) in a 'figurative non-referential' sense of 'subversive signifier displacing referent' (p. 32). Prosser says he wants to assert the specificity of 'trans' studies, as opposed to queer, precisely because of this desire for assimilation and because of what he sees as the literality/ materiality of the (trans) body. This latter point relates to the second reason for his objections to the way that transgender/ transsexuality are used in *Gender Trouble*. Butler is using queer genders as a means of revealing that the literality of heterosexuality is a performative effect, and in so doing undermines the literality of the body as causal in the subjective accounts of transsexuals. Butler's account of the performativity of the body and identity cannot, therefore, accommodate the body narratives of transsexuals, which Prosser argues instantiate the literality, or materiality, of the trans body as lived. This problem is exacerbated for Prosser as, rather than accepting this materiality as causal, Butler's account of performativity seems to work in a way that delegitimates transsexuals' pretensions to 'normal' lives. This is because it associates transgender with queer performativity in opposition to the literalizing effects of heterosexuality.

Hence, Prosser objects to what he describes as a figural/ground metaphor in *Gender Trouble* in which transgender figures gender performativity, whilst non-transgendered subjects are allocated the ground of the naturalness of sex/gender. He suggests that this 'allocates to nontransgendered subjects (according to this binary schema, straight subjects), the ground that transgender would appear only to figure' (p. 32). Moreover, he says, 'this "ground" is the apparent naturalness of sex' (p. 32) which is accorded to heterosexual identities but not to transsexuals. Prosser clearly has a valid point here. In what seems like a continuation of heterosexual privilege in Butler's own work, heterosexual identities get to fit in and belong, however performative, whilst trans identities remain queer, however adapted; they can't win in this scenario. Furthermore, and relatedly, Prosser is concerned that Butler's account of performativity amounts to a devaluing of straight gender, yet some transsexuals aspire to precisely that for themselves. He suggests that this is indicative of queers' 'sense of its own "higher purpose" ' (p. 32).

Another way of looking at this devaluing of straight gender might be to see it, not so much in terms of a 'higher purpose' as indicative of a different purpose, with different political aims. Perhaps Prosser is right to say that these differences are not commensurable. When he says Butler's account of performativity is not commensurable with transsexuals' accounts of their experiences, however, it is rather the political goals of these accounts that are not commensurable with Butler's because they conform to the binary form of sexual difference in heterosexual hegemony. Where transsexuals aim to transform their bodies to make them fit their gender, the goals of performativity involve reshaping sexual difference itself and the ways it structures the experiences of individuals; in which case the body modification, which is so crucial to transsexuality, might not matter. It is not necessarily that transsexuals' accounts of their experiences are incommensurable with performativity as a theoretical account of sexed identity, as we shall see.

One of Prosser's chief concerns is with the existence of transsexuals who, he argues, do not wish to be performative but who want 'to be constative, quite simply to be' (p. 32). However, this involves a view of the literality of the body that is simply not sustainable in Butler's account of performativity because this highlights the ways in which all identity categories, not just transgender and transsexuality, are performative effects. Butler's point is that the apparent naturalness (literality in Prosser's sense) of non-transgendered subjects is in fact an effect, a discursive, politically regulated product of the naturalization of sex and gender, which are in fact *always* performative effects. If this issue is set in the context of her discussion of the materiality of the body in the introduction to *Bodies the Matter*, it might shed further light on this matter. Butler argues that the concept of materiality is inescapably bound up with signification and that this serves to complicate traditional understandings of reference – and I might add what Prosser terms literality – 'the very meaning of "referentiality" is altered. In philosophical terms, the constative claim is always to some degree performative' (Butler 1993a: 11). This is why Butler argues that she does not so much dispute the materiality of the body as seek a genealogy of the 'normative conditions under which the materiality of the body is framed and formed, and, in particular, how it is formed through differential categories of sex' (p. 17). Drawing on transgender and transsexual identities as queering the binaries is a way of revealing the performativity of all identity categories, rather than indicating the literality of heterosexuality and the performativity of transgender.

Any apparent 'literality' is thus a performative effect of the naturalization of sex and gender. In *Gender Trouble* the focus is on the way that gender could be seen to be a productive principle in the performative production of sexed identity. In *Bodies that Matter* this is rethought with more attention to the category of 'sex' as a productive principle – but neither is regarded as a generative ground in the sense that Prosser wants to retain in relation to the literality of transsexuals' bodies. Butler is arguing that what is taken to be a generative ground in heterosexual contexts is also a performative effect, but it takes a focus on the excluded aspects in that principle of literalization to highlight this: i.e. those mismatches between bodily categories and gender identity that are apparent in transgender and transsexual contexts. Thus, where Prosser argues that there is a binary of 'heterosexual = literalizing/queer = performative' (Prosser 1998: 48) at work in *Gender Trouble* that continues to be evident in *Bodies that Matter* (though not without changes in the understanding of transsexuality), it might be better to describe this as heterosexuality = literalizing/queer = deliteralizing.[6] This would more closely represent Butler's aims in this work.

Butler aims to show that all identity, whether queer, straight or trans, is performatively produced and no-one can simply 'be' outside of this process, as Prosser suggests transsexuals would like think of themselves. However, even if they were to accept this fundamental insight, the problem that still remains for Prosser, and transsexuals who want to fit in and belong, is that the account of performativity in *Gender Trouble* and *Bodies that Matter* seems to be emphsizing the literalizing effects of heterosexuality in opposition to the deliteralizing effects of

transgender. This would seem to place transsexuals in an unwelcome double bind and an unwelcome political position of destabilizing the binaries. At the same time, and most importantly,
it involves a deliteralization of the categories of sex that Prosser
wants to retain as necessary to, and demonstrated in, transsexuals' narratives. (Despite the fact that this apparent literality
is unintelligible to both trans and others without modification.)

This brings us to the third reason why Prosser objects to
Butler's account of the performativity of sex and gender. He
takes exception to the way in which the idea that sex somehow
causes gender is reversed in 'Prohibition, Psychoanalysis, and
the Production of the Heterosexual Matrix' (in *Gender Trouble*)
to become gender somehow causing sex or sex as 'gender all
along'. Prosser is concerned about the implications that this
reversal has for theorizing transsexual subjectivities, especially
in relation to transsexuals' own sense of interiority as a driving
force for their sexed identity. What he objects to in particular is
that Butler's reading of Freud and psychoanalysis 'refigures sex
from material corporeality into phantasized surface; and through
this it reinscribes the opposition between queer and heterosexual already at work in *Gender Trouble*, sustaining it by once
again enlisting transgender as queer' (Prosser 1998: 40).

Prosser thus takes issue with Butler's reading of Freud's reference to the ego as 'first and foremost a bodily ego' (which is
discussed in Chapter 3) to make her argument about the body
as morphology. In this reading any feelings of sexed or gendered
interiority become phantasmatic effects. However, Prosser claims
that Butler puts too much emphasis on surface as that which
produces interiority through disciplinary practices and, in so
doing, occludes any role for interiority; and that transsexual
narratives undermine this view, precisely because they are based
on a notion of interiority. He argues:

> The transsexual doesn't necessarily *look* differently gen-
> dered, but by definition *feels* differently gendered from her
> or his birth-assigned sex. In both its medical and its auto-
> biographical versions, the transsexual narrative depends
> upon an initial crediting of this feeling as generative ground.
> It demands some recognition of the category of corporeal
> interiority (internal bodily sensations) and of its distinctive-

ness from that which can be seen (external surface): the difference between gender identity and sex that serves as the logic of transsexuality.

(Prosser 1998: 44, original emphasis)

Prosser argues forcibly that Butler's account of performativity simply ignores this difference, and rejects her view of transsexuality as exemplifying the phantasmatic status of sex (in the one place that transsexuality is mentioned in *Gender Trouble*). He argues that it is rather that transsexuals' experience of their bodies as sexed in opposition to their apparent external materiality is consistent with Freud's idea of a bodily ego in a material rather than phantasmatic sense. He argues that the fact that the imaginary body is spoken of as 'more real or more sensible', in transsexuals' own testimonies, 'illustrates the materiality of the bodily ego rather than the phantasmatic status of the sexed body: the material reality of the imaginary and not, as Butler would have it, the imaginariness of material reality' (p. 44).

However, the problem with this view is that transsexuals' (interior) sense of the material reality of their bodies' sexed nature (their sexed self) is at variance with their apparent biological categorization (nature), so whilst it might seem to be the cause of the transsexuals' sense of identity in their own stories and, as such, located within the body, it isn't clear how this causal relation is generated in the bodies' materiality: how these feelings of interiority are generated in opposition to their apparent (external) material reality, if indeed that materiality is causal but doesn't fit the external categorization. So, in this sense, doesn't the material reality of the imaginary to which Prosser refers rather support Butler's view of the imaginariness of material reality, precisely because that material reality in its interiority is at variance with the external aspect of that material reality?

Furthermore, Prosser argues that it is the very fact 'that sex is perceived as something that must be changed [that] underlines its very unphantasmatic status' (p. 44). However, it could be argued that the reverse of this argument, which is more in keeping with Butler's account, makes more sense for the same reason: precisely because it is felt it must be changed underlines the phantasmatic status of the feeling. In addition, whilst it is impossible to adjudicate on Freud's views on the matter of the bodily ego, it is nevertheless a defining feature of psychoanalysis that any somatic aspects of identity are never immediate. So whilst Butler builds on this insight in ways that Prosser wants to argue are undermined in transsexuals' accounts of their bodily being, this is not necessarily the case if the mediation of those feelings is taken into account, through what Butler describes as 'compulsory heterosexuality' and 'phallocentrism' or, indeed, heterosexual hegemony, which all work to constitute subjectivities (and feelings of interiority) as unintelligible in other than binary terms. This is not to suggest some sort of dualism of mind and body here, but rather to indicate the impossibility of knowing the body outside of particular, historically specific, conceptual frameworks: that what we take to be immediate truly never can be.

Hence, Prosser argues that denying the body any role in the construction of identity cannot account for the role that trans people feel that their bodies play in their experience of transsexuality. He argues that the 'body narratives of transsexuals give testimony to the materiality of the body' and reveal that 'embodiment is as much about feeling one inhabits material flesh as the flesh itself' (p. 7). He takes the view that the experience of transsexuality belies Butler's account of the materiality of the body as a cultural product because the resistance to cultural construction seems to stem from the materiality of the transsexual's own body. Surgical realignment to produce a match between the transsexual's sense of their gender identity and their biological body is regarded by Prosser as necessary to establish a 'real' gender identity, to taking them 'home'. Although this view of a 'real' gender identity has been criticized (Halberstam 1998) and he has since modified his views on this matter (Prosser 1999), the issue of the role of the materiality of the body that Prosser identifies could be interpreted in a way that is in keeping with Butler's account of performativity.

It is possible that, rather than it being the body in its materiality that causes individual transsexuals to seek surgical realignment (so that their biological body matches their gender identity and they come 'home'), it is the production of their bodies as unintelligible *even to themselves* within the heterosexual imaginary which produces the desire for sex reassignment surgery, to 'belong'. That the need for body modification does not arise for those transgendered individuals who are willing to challenge existing categorizations (e.g. Stone 1991; Halberstam 1998) would seem to support this view. Moreover, this could shed some light on the reason why surgical realignment works – or not. It could be that it works, when it does, precisely because it was not the biological body that caused the performance of gender as Butler insists, so that the individual concerned has indeed, if not come 'home', at least become intelligible to themselves and thereby feels as if they have come home. On the other hand, perhaps it fails, when it does, precisely because even post-operative transsexual bodies, if visible as such, remain abject in a cultural framework that is governed by the heterosexual imaginary – even as their existence contributes, however reluctantly, to the productive crisis that Butler would hope to occur. Hence, the need to displace the heterosexual imaginary that lies at the core of Butler's queer feminist theory. Without this, and despite the gains brought by the Gender Recognition Act 2004 in the UK, trans people may well continue to occupy abject subject positions; and to live not only with the symbolic violence involved in the heterosexual imaginary but also the threat of physical violence and even murder, as in the plight of Teena Brandon and Venus Xtravaganza.[7]

Furthermore, and most significantly, whilst Butler's account of performativity involves the rejection of any notion of the materiality of the body as generative principle, it does not impugn the significance of the materiality of the body as lived. It is rather a way of showing how that significance is a product of signification and systems of meaning and power. In this sense it could be argued that it wasn't the literality of Venus Xtravaganza's body that resulted in her death (during the course of the filming of *Paris is Burning*) as Prosser contends, so much as the meaning of that literality in the context of heterosexual hegemony (and turning tricks), not to mention 'race' and class.[8]

Imaginary bodies and sexual difference

Prosser's arguments about the centrality of the material body to trans experiences and identity in some ways parallel feminists concerns about the significance of the materiality of female bodies, even when there is broad acceptance of the significance of the social constitution of identity and the impossibility of accessing the body 'as such' outside of particular modes of conceptualization. Biddy Martin, for example, argues that even if there is no way of getting at our bodily experiences outside of cultural frameworks and signification, it is still necessary to maintain a sense of the materiality of the body as some kind of limit otherwise 'the all-too-obvious and thus invisible difference that it makes to be a woman drops out of view' (Martin 1994: 112), as discussed in Chapter 2. She argues 'that we pay more respect to what's given, to limits, even as we open the future to what is now unthinkable or delegitimated, that we do this in order to generate a notion of difference that is not fixed or stable in its distribution across bodies, but is also not dispensable' (p. 112).

This concern is also echoed in the work of Grosz (1994, 1995) and Gatens (1996). They, like Butler, want to rethink the materiality of the body without involving any kind of biological reductionism. However, in contrast to Butler, they want to retain some sort of role for the body in the formation of identity. Their arguments draw on the psychoanalytic concept of the imaginary as well as phenomenological approaches to the body as lived. They involve the view that becoming an embodied subject involves a kind of internal image or corporeal schema, which is a social and cultural product through which any apparently simply natural or biological aspect is experienced. The salience of the specificities of women's bodies to their subjectivity can then be accommodated alongside the recognition that every aspect of women's bodies is necessarily socially and culturally mediated, including biology itself. An emphasis on the significance of sexual difference to body image and in the experience of bodies as lived is thus retained. In this way the body does remain some kind of drag on signification, as Martin suggests that it should.

The trouble with these accounts, however, lies in the way they accept sexual difference as in some sense immutable. Grosz, for example, provides a powerful analysis of the ways in which the conceptualization of corporeality has tied women to their apparently biological natures whilst freeing men from theirs. She argues forcefully that recognizing the centrality of the body to subjectivity, for both women and men, requires rethinking the matter of the body beyond the binary thinking of mind/body dualism, material/culture, sex/gender. Grosz nevertheless insists that an always present sexual difference be recognized and it is that which provides the conditions of possibility for the process of embodiment. She does not mean by this to imply that the meaning and content of sexual difference is given in any way, including biologically, 'naturally' or psychologically. Instead she suggests it is to be thought of as an alterity that provides the conditions of possibility for embodiment. 'Sexual difference is the horizon that cannot appear in its own terms but is implied in the very possibility of an entity, an identity, a subject, an other and their relations' (Grosz 1994: 209). From the perspective of Butler's account of performativity this may be so, but that it *should* be so is something that bears questioning.

Hence, Grosz's rethinking of subjectivity as corporeal, her recognition that subjectivity is embodied and her attempt at rethinking and revaluing women's bodies are all premised on an acceptance of the irreducibility of sexual difference rather than seeing sexual difference itself as a product of regimes of power/ knowledge that shape, and are shaped by, the social institution of heterosexuality. Butler's account of performativity and the materialization of the body allows us to see this. Furthermore, this view would seem to be corroborated by the experiences of transsexual and transgender individuals whose situation cannot be accommodated in the binary notion of sexual difference, and whose subjectivity is clearly not based on the kind of body image or corporeal schema suggested in accounts based on the irreducibility of sexual difference. Indeed, Grosz's insistence that male-to-female transsexuals are not women because they cannot feel like women would seem to be based on a sort of essentialist view of the link between body processes, however conceived, and sex/gender. This view is also problematized by the fact that many mtf transsexuals go through radical surgery precisely because, as they insist, they do feel like a woman. The rejection of mtf transsexuals as women, then, highlights much of what is problematic with these approaches. That such bodies may not be entitled to be included in the category women and are rather regarded as 'posing women' indicates that a kind of binary bodily givenness is involved. Despite Grosz's attempt to rethink the sex/gender distinction and her recognition of the biological body as mediated, indeed culturally constituted, matter, her rethinking of corporeality still rests ultimately on the indispensability of sexual difference as given in binary terms.

Precisely because in Butler's account there is a refusal to accept a notion of sexual difference as given, and it is conceived instead as socially instituted to function as given, it is not accepted as something which is in some sense immutable or indispensable which provides a limit to the process of social construction, as these accounts suggest. This would be to continue the binary thinking that Butler's account of performativity seeks to challenge. As she concedes in one interview, there is a limit to constructedness but just what that limit is remains unspecifiable (Meijer and Prins 1998: 28). Although Butler develops a notion of constraint in *Bodies that Matter*, this concerns only the 'constitutive constraints' involved in the symbolic demand to take up sexed positions, and the repudiations and exclusions involved in this. It does not allow the consideration of the kind of constraints that Gatens, Grosz or Martin are suggesting, any more than it considers constraints that result from biological or physiological features; or what Alsop *et al.* describe as 'the material reality', 'the brute material features' (Alsop *et al.* 2002: 177) which, they argue, enable the naturalizing of the various constructions in particular social imaginaries (as discussed in Chapter 2). This is because, from the perspective of performativity, it can be recognized that any particular material reality becomes so only through a process of materialization. Indeed, its depiction as a foundation waiting to be given expression is part of the very process of that materialization. There are many examples in the history and philosophy of science that demonstrate the importance of conceptual frameworks and cultural values in interpreting what is 'seen', what is apparently simply 'there' in the world, just as there are in physics and in anthropology. These demonstrate how what is at one time considered a 'brute' materiality turns into something quite different in a new conceptual framework.[9] Butler's account of the body as a performative effect goes some way to explaining how this works in relation to the materialization of bodies as objects in the world for others, and our subjective experience of them in terms of their sexed materiality and the duality of sexual difference.

Conclusion

Whilst the possibility of moving beyond binary thinking on sexual difference seems wildly unthinkable or, if anything, utopian in a hegemonic system that privileges heterosexuality, it is clear that Butler's account of performativity presents a challenge to the duality of sexual difference and the binary system of sex and gender that it sustains. Making sense of the bodies of trans individuals involves rethinking the categories of sex, gender, sexuality and the body beyond the binary frame, and thus has significant implications for feminist body theory. In particular, trans experiences seem to undermine accounts of the body that are based on imaginary schemata that are rooted in the duality of sexual difference which is somehow given in the materiality of the body. However, this is not to suggest that trans experiences open up a conceptual space between male and female. Although this may lend a greater, and much needed, intelligibility to trans bodies and trans identities, it would still seem to accord a sort of (bodily) propriety to maleness and femaleness which, it has been argued, is in fact undermined by those experiences and by Butler's account of sexual difference as a performative effect. It has been argued instead that trans experiences could contribute in some way to what Butler describes as the 'remapping of sexual difference' and could thus contribute towards rearticulating the hegemonic symbolic in a non-binary form.

Whether it will do this is another matter, as the precise route to change and transformation is unpredictable in the kind of theoretical framework that is involved in Butler's work. Nevertheless, this is not to undermine the challenge that these insights present to feminist theorizing on the basis of sexual difference. Furthermore, it could be that, by giving credence to the idea that there is no necessity to the duality of sexual difference, whether in an ontological, epistemological or indeed experiential sense, and instead refusing to accept the irreducibility of sexual difference in any sense, feminist theorizing could also contribute to the reformulation of sexual difference and the hegemonic symbolic in other than binary terms.

Afterword

In this book, I have attempted to provide a critical analysis of Butler's work on sex, gender, sexuality and the body through an examination of the development of her account of performativity and its precursors, both feminist and non-feminist. Particular attention has been given to the relationship between language and materiality, especially in relation to the materiality of the body, the issue of agency and political practice, and the possibility of social change and transformation. This is because the promise of Butler's influential theoretical moves is the least obvious in these areas and they have attracted the most criticism from feminist and queer commentators. In examining these criticisms, I have tried to provide a nuanced assessment of the positive and negative implications of understanding identity categories and the bodies of individuals as performative effects. Particular attention has also been paid to the issue of sexual difference and the significance of this for understanding subjectivity, identity and the body.

If at times I have presented Butler's ideas in ways that would seem to go against the grain of one of the key theoretical insights of her approach, which emphasizes the problems of determining 'proper objects', this has been done in the interests of exposition. It is not intended to undermine those insights in any way, or to assert 'proper objects' in relation to Butler's work, but rather to provide a starting point from which to begin to engage with it.

To the extent that Butler's account of materiality as a matter of materialization presents a radical view of bodies, subjectivities and selves, it seems hard to reconcile it with the everyday experiences of these aspects of bodily being; their apparent materiality and givenness, here in the world. Nevertheless, I have tried to show that Butler's account of performativity does little, if anything, to challenge the materiality of that givenness as felt experience, but rather seeks to show how that very felt experience and givenness are far from immediate but are also a product of materiality: the materiality of the significatory processes which provide the possibility for any kind of experience, any kind of matter to come into being at all. Particular attention has been paid to what this might mean for feminist and trans theory in relation to the implications it has for understanding the materiality of the body, sex and gender, as well as for agency and political practice, social change and transformation.

Although I have tried to avoid so-called 'jargon' as much as possible, sometimes it just has to be faced. The very mention of a term such as 'significatory processes' is enough to make some people switch off. Nevertheless such a term is required to try to convey the intricate complexity of the interweaving of language, signs and symbols, matter, bodies, psyches, subjectivities, identities, differences, imaginaries and practices which provide the conditions of possibility, in a Foucauldian sense, for contemporary life and experience as we know it. It is hoped that this book will help to clarify the significance of these matters for those who are sceptical.

Despite his emphasis on resistance, Foucault's genealogical analyses cannot explain theoretically how it is that individuals are never entirely determined by the disciplinary power that constitutes them.[1] I have argued that Butler's account of performativity addresses this problem by combining speech act theory with a psychoanalytic concept of the psyche, and reading both of these through a Foucauldian account of power and normalization, subjectivity and subjection – particularly, as all this is set in the context of Althusser's account of interpellation, Derrida's critique of presence, and Nietzsche's critique of the metaphysics of substance. Adapting Foucault's application of Nietzschean genealogy to the feminist and queer problematic of sex, gender, sexuality and the body, read through aspects of psychoanalysis, is a brilliant and creative move that surely amounts to a paradigm shift in gender theory, as well as making a founding contribution to queer theory. Its influence on feminist theory is far-reaching and it has surely revolutionized gender studies, not least in that Butler's focus on the epistemological and ontological significance of phallogocentrism and heterosexual hegemony in the production of sexed identity has highly significant implications in each of these fields. It also has important methodological implications for social research. Although this account of performativity has potentially devastating implications for some feminist theories that base their accounts on the materiality of women's experience and bodies; and for identity politics based on commonality and sameness, at the same time it alerts us to the vested interests and power relations involved in particular constitutions of that experience. Indeed, it is clear that in many ways Butler's account of performativity extends the earlier radical feminist slogan 'The personal is political' and contributes enormously to the further development of feminist frameworks for understanding experience.

Most significantly, Butler's work highlights the crucial role that heterosexual hegemony plays in the naturalization of performatively instituted gender identities and power relations, and calls attention to practices of masculinity and femininity as constitutive of sexed and gendered identities. In this sense, as well as having enormous significance for feminist theory and practice and for queer theory, it also contributes to critical masculinity studies, which have developed in opposition to the growth of an uncritical men's studies, as an offshoot of gender studies.[2] Moreover, performativity also provides a means of understanding other aspects of identity, such as 'race', 'ethnicity' and class, as 'vectors of power' rather than properties of bodies or particular groups or individuals. Whilst the power relations and symbolic operations involved in these aspects of identity are not necessarily analogous to those at work in the institution of sex and gender, it is clear that they are equally significant and also articulated with these aspects (and thus heterosexual hegemony) in their performative production.

Butler's account of performativity also has significant political implications, although the issue of political adequacy is one of the most problematic areas of her work. Whilst Butler insists on the political relevance of her work and describes herself as 'a theorist of political strategy' (Meijer and Prins 1998: 276), her account of performativity is criticized as politically debilitating if there is no independently existing body on which to base feminist and queer projects and there are no independent truths of sex, gender and sexuality on which to build identity, including trans identity, not even the duality of sexual difference. Moreover, the view that there is no subject who precedes action but that subjects are constituted in and through their actions, which underpins Butler's critique of identity and account of performativity, is also a radical and counter-intuitive view (rooted in the work of Nietzsche, Derrida and Foucault). This view of the subject would seem to undermine the very possibility of agency.

However, I have argued, with Butler, that these features of her account do not necessarily undermine the possibility of any kind of political practice or agency. It is rather that they indicate the need for political recognition of these 'facts' and the inadequacy of traditional understandings of the political, and political practice, which take traditional understandings of the subject as given. They indicate the inadequacy of accounts of agency rooted in the structure of the humanist subject. Butler's account of performativity provides a way of theorizing the significance of all this for rethinking sex, gender and sexuality. It also provides a starting point for rethinking these aspects in other than binary terms, even if it doesn't seem possible to move beyond them. Furthermore, it provides an account of agency that doesn't depend on the idea of a humanist subject but instead shows the limitations of this understanding of agency for social change and transformation. Thus, whilst the effectivity of Butler's view of agency as a political strategy is called into question because it is concerned with resistance rather than providing a programmatic vision for feminist political practice, or, indeed, any other form of political practice, precisely because of the view of change and transformation that it involves. The analysis in this book has tried to show that this inability is not so much a weakness of Butler's approach, as a recognition of the limitations of any such 'programmatic vision' and the unpredictability and contingency of large-scale political programmes. Furthermore, it calls attention to the violence and exclusions on which any kind of identity politics is based.

Notes

Introduction

1 The backdrop to Butler's work on gender was her earlier interrogation of Hegel, Marx and German idealism which involved a visit to Germany to study Hegel and hermeneutics on a Fulbright scholarship. Her first book *Subjects of Desire* (Butler 1987a) set these concerns in the context of French thinkers such as Derrida and Foucault, as she says in the interview with Liz Kotz (Kotz and Butler 1992).

2 See, for example, Butler's discussion of these and other methodological issues in 'Against Proper Objects' (Butler 1994b). This was the introductory essay to a special issue of *differences* which examined the relationship between feminism and queer theory. Butler discusses this relationship, drawing out the problems of boundaries and methodological distinctions, and emphasizes the links between feminism and lesbian and gay studies. For further discussion of the debates within feminism, and/or between feminists and queer theorists, about whether the focus of analysis should be gender or sex and sexuality, see Alsop *et al.* (2002), Merck *et al.* (1998).

1 Gender as performance and performative

1 This notion of performing identity has been taken up and applied in a number of studies, particularly in the context of performing lesbian and gay male identity. See, for example, Bell *et al.* (1994), Kaplan (1992), Weston (1993), Koestenbaum (1991), Esterberg (1996). It has also been widely criticized, e.g. by Tyler (1991), Walker (1995) and Lloyd (1999).

2 Nietzsche's critique of the 'metaphysics of substance' is discussed in *Gender Trouble* (see especially pp. 16–23) and *Bodies that Matter*.

3 That this interpretation of Goffman might be disputed is another matter; the point remains the same.

4 Epstein (1996) and Namaste (1996) are both included in Seidman

(ed.) (1996). This collection provides an early discussion of the intersection of sociology and queer theory. Several of the papers discuss aspects of Butler's work.

5 Butler asks this question herself (Butler 1988: 526; 1990a: 140).

6 Although Butler becomes increasingly concerned with the psychic aspects of identity as she develops her notion of performativity in *The Psychic Life of Power* (1997b) (which is discussed in Chapter 2), her account of performativity in *Gender Trouble* does not yet involve psychoanalytic explanations in its attempt to accommodate interior features of the self whilst avoiding essentialist understandings.

7 Monique Wittig was one of the founding editors of the journal *Questions Féministes* (translated as *Feminist Issues*). The journal represented a rather different materialist feminist position to that of Butler. Butler discusses this difference in *Gender Trouble*. She contrasts Wittig's view of the 'mark of gender' and role of language as a tool of heterosexist oppression with Irigaray's post-Lacanian psychoanalytic view. For Wittig, following Colette Guillaumin's work on the mark of race, and Simone de Beauvoir's account of women as the 'second sex', only women are marked by gender, and this mark serves to differentiate them from men and thus deny them the status of a fully fledged person. For Irigaray, the feminine is never a mark of gender as it is rather the signification of a lack 'produced by a set of differentiating linguistic rules that effectively create sexual difference' (Butler 1990a: 27). See especially Butler's discussion of the workings of the metaphysics of substance (pp. 16–27).

8 Like Irigaray, Derrida also employs the term 'phallogocentrism' at times to indicate the sexual structure of the metaphysics of presence.

9 The question of foundations is also discussed in Butler (1992a).

10 Indeed, not only has the notion of a universal self been revealed by feminist enquiry to be andocentric, but it has also been shown to be ethnocentric.

11 Ziarek (1997) makes a similar point.

2 Body matters: from construction to materialization

1 Despite certain earlier attempts to argue otherwise (Butler 1986, 1987b).

2 These contexts include philosophical and psychoanalytic writings, essays in sexual theory and politics, as well as literary texts and novels, the film *Paris is Burning*, and the radical democratic theory of Slavoj Žižek.

3 See for example 'Phantasmatic Identification and the Assumption of Sex', 'Gender is Burning' and the discussion of Nella Larsen's *Passing* in *Bodies that Matter* (Butler 1993a). 'Race' is considered as a vector of power rather than a bodily basis of identity and the

intersection of gender and sexual regulation with racial regulation is examined, especially in the latter. Indeed, Butler contends that 'it seems crucial to rethink the scenes of reproduction and hence of sexing practices not only as ones through which a heterosexual imperative is inculcated, but as ones through which boundaries of racial distinction are secured as well as contested' (Butler 1993a: 18).

4 For a further discussion of this see Jagger (2001).

5 Butler (1992a) discusses the use of poststructuralism for considering violence to women's bodies in 'Contingent Foundations: Feminism and the Question of Postmodernism', which forms the introduction to *Feminists Theorize the Political* (Butler and Scott 1992). (See in particular pp. 17–19. See also Marcus (1992) 'Fighting Bodies, Fighting Words: A Theory and Politics of Rape' in the same collection.)

6 'Logocentrism' is a term used by Derrida (1974, 1982) to characterize the Western philosophical tradition. He uses it to suggest that this is based on a myth of presence (as discussed earlier) which is organized around an illusory centre which privileges the immediacy of speech over the written word. His deconstruction of the speech writing/opposition aims to show that when speech is also recognized as a form of 'writing', as discussed here, and placed in the context of *différance*, this myth is no longer sustainable.

7 Foucault himself was aware of these difficulties. Perhaps because of them, he switched his attention from the body/subject to the problematic of the self in his later works, where he attempted to formulate an 'aesthetics of existence', leaving various problems in this area unanswered.

8 A similar point is made by Shildrick (1997) in her notion of *Leaky Bodies*. Shildrick also draws on Derrida's notion of 'writing' and *différance*. As she argues in relation to bioethics,

'Once real material bodies as well as linguistic concepts are understood to be discursive constructions, then the practices of medicine and health care can be seen in a different light' (Shildrick 1997: 12). Hence, it's not only that bodily concepts such as 'notions of health and disease, able-bodied and disabled, and so on, become problematic, but that bio-medicine may be concerned as much with constituting the body as with restoring it' (p. 12). In other words, the extent to which bioethics, which ostensibly bears merely a regulatory role, is implicated in the *production* of bodies as biological entities can then be seen. From the perspective of 'writing' and *différance*, it is not only that bodies are not simply given in discourse or nature, but rather that they can *never* be fixed or sealed and as such are 'leaky'. Playing on the notion of leakiness – which is a characteristic traditionally accorded to (permeable) female, rather than (impermeable) male, bodies (Grosz 1994) – Shildrick argues that leakiness is an intrinsic aspect of all bodies. She argues that Derrida's concepts of 'writing' and *différance* help to reveal that.

9 In *Gender Trouble* Butler questions Freud's assumption of the role
of primary masculine and feminine dispositions that are involved
in the repudiation of opposite-sex identification in the Oedipal
complex. She argues that these are implicitly premised on a heterosexual understanding of desire, in which opposites attract. She
asks 'to what extent do we read desire for the father as evidence of
a feminine disposition only because we begin, despite the postulation of primary bisexuality, with a heterosexual matrix for desire?'
(Butler 1990a: 60). This would seem to be evident in Freud's conceptualization of a primary bisexuality which is based on the existence of both feminine and masculine dispositions as defined in
heterosexuality. The object of the masculine disposition is never
the father and the object of the feminine disposition is never the
mother. This understanding of bisexuality therefore doesn't involve
any same-sex desire but is still based on heterosexuality. It implies
that 'for Freud *bisexuality is the coincidence of two heterosexual
desires within a single psyche*' (p. 60, original emphasis).
10 Butler also discusses her relation to sexual difference theorists in an
interview with Braidotti (Braidotti with Butler 1994).
11 For a discussion of the ways in which Butler's theoretical perspective
differs from Derrida's, see Kirby (1997).
12 Derrida was always less inclined to refer to his critique of presence,
différance, or, indeed, deconstruction as strategies. Nevertheless,
this hasn't stopped others from viewing them, and using them,
in this way.
13 Butler (1993a) also points out that her focus on the materialization
of bodies in *Bodies that Matter* is a function of her own interest in
developing a critique of identity in relation to sexuality and sexual
difference, but this doesn't mean that this is the only framework
through which bodies are materialized. It doesn't mean that sexual
difference is any more primary than other forms of difference either,
but that the heterosexual imperative is 'interarticulated' with other
vectors of power in the materialization of bodies and the production of sexed identities, sexed materiality. Examples might be 'race'
and 'ethnicity', class, age, ability/disability. (See also the debate
mentioned below; Butler 1995a.)
14 This 'debate' is essentially a discussion setting out and defending
the theoretical positions of the four protagonists. There is a particular focus on the question of agency and the intricacies of Butler's
and Cornell's differing theoretical allegiances to poststructuralism.

3 Performativity, subjection and the possibility of agency

1 Butler also discusses Foucault's lack of attention to the role of
exclusion and erasures in the discursive construction of sexed identities in 'Sexual Inversions' (Butler 1992b). In this paper she develops
her critique of Foucault on this matter by reading his account of the

fictionality of 'sex' as a principle of identity, through aspects of Irigaray's work, in which the focus is on the exclusion of the feminine in the production of coherent identities.

2 See Lloyd (1999) for a useful critique of the political possibilities of voluntarist interpretations of Butler's account of gender performativity.

3 Butler makes this critique in a section in *Gender Trouble* entitled 'Freud and the Melancholy of Gender', where she analyses Freud's views on the character formation of the ego through a process of internalization, as expressed in 'Mourning and Melancholia'. Although she rereads Freud, and reformulates the process of internalization as a matter of psychic incorporation, to develop her account of the melancholic structure of gender in the *Psychic Life of Power*, her critique of the separation of identification and desire in psychoanalytic theories still stands. She argues that this separation amounts to a 'false foundationalism' rooted in normative heterosexuality.

4 Indeed, the articulation of the psyche and the social is an aspect that is not adequately addressed in the work of either Freud or Lacan, neither of whom seems able to account adequately for the social and historical aspects of their accounts. For example, with hindsight, it can be seen that although Freud based his account of Oedipal relations on a version of the patriarchal family that is culturally and historically specific, it would seem that he failed to recognize this and did not develop those aspects of his work that could accommodate it. Lacan separates the psychic and the social, the symbolic and the empirical historical realm, and therefore renders his account ahistorical and inevitable; in this way, it is argued, he does not leave the space for change.

5 In this collection Butler, Laclau and Žižek debate the significance of identity formation for radical democratic politics, each author addressing the criticisms the others make of their ideas and highlighting the similarities and differences in their adaptation of psychoanalytic insights. The debate takes the form of a jointly authored introduction and three sets of questions, one from each author, followed by nine individually authored chapters, three from each theorist. Individual chapters are cited, where appropriate, in the following discussion.

6 See also Butler's analysis of *Antigone* (Butler 2000c).

7 Butler's analysis of Antigone (Butler 2000c) is cited as an acknowledgement of those whose relations are still not accepted as a matter of legitimate kinship, showing how a culture of normative heterosexuality obstructs the capacity to see what sexual freedom and political agency could be, and foreclosing other possibilities.

8 In some ways these debates echo the sociological problem of the relationship between structure and agency. Butler's account of interpellation through melancholic incorporation contributes

usefully to the current impasse in sociological theory on this matter by demonstrating that the structural roots of the psychic aspects of identity are in fact social in origin. This insight is of considerable significance for theorizing the social construction of 'race' and 'ethnicity', as well as gender (see also Chapter 4).

4 The politics of the performative: hate speech, pornography and 'race'

1 For a useful discussion of sexual innuendo as an example of excitable speech and a possible site of political resistance, see Failler (2005). The focus on sexual innuendo is particularly useful because it relies explicitly on what is unsaid as much as what is said for its meaning to be effective. That such a reliance is always present as an unacknowledged foundation in the operations of language and signification is one of the founding assumptions of poststructuralism. Much of Butler's work involves making that reliance explicit.

2 Butler acknowledges this debt to Derrida in a number of places in *Excitable Speech*, and discusses the significance of it in particular in her critique of Bourdieu in 'Implicit Censorship and Discursive Agency' (which is included as Chapter 4).

3 Butler makes an intricate analysis of Althusser's account of the ideological constitution of the subject through the divine power of naming in 'Ideology and Ideological State Apparatuses'. It is difficult to do justice to this here (see especially pp. 31–4).

4 In 'Implicit Censorship and Discursive Agency' (Chapter 4 of *Excitable Speech*), Butler contrasts Derrida's view of the performativity of speech acts as inherently iterative, and thus necessarily breaking with prior contexts, with what she identifies as Bourdieu's more static account of the force of the performative lying in the workings of social ritual. Indeed, she suggests that this aspect of Derrida's work 'offers an important counterpoint to functionalist social theory' (Butler 1997a: 182, n. 32).

5 Butler is careful to point out that this is a rhetorical reading rather than a legal interpretation of the reasoning (see also Butler 1997a: 171, n. 16). However, that she clearly does not want to suggest that there are legal flaws in the arguments is perhaps the most salient point. These arguments are legally sound despite the implicit racism of the decisions, and the explicit anti–racism of the US state.

6 The rioting in Los Angeles referred to here is that which followed the decision of a court in Simi Valley to acquit four policemen of brutally beating a black man, whose name was Rodney King, despite video evidence of the event. Butler suggests that an alternative reading is that this rioting could be said to have been 'sparked' by the decision in order to challenge 'whether the claim of having been injured can be heard and countenanced by a jury and judge who are extremely susceptible to the suggestion that a black person

is always and only endangering, never endangered' (Butler 1997a: 59). See also Butler (1993b) 'Endangered/Endangering: Schematic Racism and White Paranoia'. Here Butler provides what she describes in a footnote as 'a strategically aggressive counter-reading' (p. 22) of the video recording and, the Simi Valley jury's failure to find the police officers involved guilty of using excessive force. She suggests that this failure to 'see' the excessive force is a product of 'the racist schema that orchestrates and interprets the event, which splits the violent intention off from the body who wields it and attributes it to the body who receives it' (p. 20). She argues that this is because the racist schema is permeated by 'white paranoia'. The black body of Rodney King is therefore conceived in terms of danger and threat. So the raising of a hand in what would seem, on an alternative reading, to be a natural act of self-protection against the onslaught of blows to the head, comes to be seen rather as a threat of violence. The violent actions of the police thus become a matter of protecting the white bodies outside the police circle at the scene and in the rest of Simi Valley from the black threat within. Hence the responsibility for the violence is perceived to lie in King's own hands. Butler suggests that if the raising of his hand in this context can be interpreted as evidence of King's control of the scene and 'threatening intentions then a circuit is phantasmatically produced whereby King is the origin, the intention, the object of the selfsame' (p. 20). Butler suggests that the rioting that followed the verdict (in which a number of black people were killed by the police), and the media reporting of it (for example as 'senseless' and 'barbaric'), and commentary on it, served to reiterate the 'reversal and displacement of dangerous intention' (p. 21) involved in the circuit of white racist violence.

7 For a further discussion of Dworkin and MacKinnon's campaign against pornography and the debates within feminism around these very complex issues, see Cornell (2000) and Itzin (1992).

8 See 'The Force of Fantasy: Feminism, Mapplethorpe, and Discursive Excess' (Butler 1990b) for an earlier discussion of the significance of Mapplethorpe's work.

9 See 'Contagious Word: Paranoia and "Homosexuality" in the Military' (Chapter 3 of *Excitable Speech*).

10 For a discussion and critique of Habermas in *Excitable Speech*, see pp. 86–9.

5 Beyond identity politics: gender, transgender and sexual difference

1 The term 'trans' is employed in a broad sense to include transgender, transsexuality and all forms of gender crossing that fall outside of the binary gender system. See Stryker (1994) and Heyes (2003)

for a discussion of the significance of terminology, and Prosser (1998) for an argument against this usage.

2 See for example, Bornstein (1994), Epstein and Straub (1991), Halberstam (1998, 2001), Stryker and Whittle (2006), Whittle (2002), and Wilchins (1997) for some insightful discussions on this matter.

3 For example, Namaste (1996) criticizes Butler for suggesting that transsexuals at the drag balls were involved in 'an uncritical miming of the hegemonic understanding of gender'. See also More (1999) for an interview with Butler on the subject of transsexuality.

4 See Chapters 1 and 4 of this book.

5 For an interesting discussion of transsexuality and psychoanalysis see Morgan (1999).

6 Prosser suggests that: 'If in *Gender Trouble* the transsexual is not distinguished from the queer transgendered subject, in *Bodies that Matter* the transsexual is specifically elected as the subject who most succinctly illustrates the limitations of the queerness of transgender' (Prosser 1998: 44–5).

7 Venus Xtravaganza was a pre-operative Latino transsexual who was taking part in a docudrama, *Paris is Burning*. Venus was found dead in the course of the filming whilst apparently turning tricks to earn money for her operation. The film, and Butler's seminal readings of it in *Gender Trouble* and *Bodies that Matter*, have been the subject of much controversy. The story of Teena Brandon's life and murder in December 1993 is portrayed in the film *Boys Don't Cry* (1999). S/he tried to pass as a man and was also attacked and brutally killed.

8 Whilst Butler's account of performativity in *Gender Trouble* and *Bodies that Matter* may not explain the feelings of interiority that in the body narratives of transsexuals cause their transsexuality, any more than the apparent interiority of other identities, whether homosexual or heterosexual, she does address the issue of interiority further in the *Psychic Life of Power* (which is discussed in Chapter 3).

9 Indeed, Fausto-Sterling (2000) provides a now classic example of the significance of existing conceptual frameworks in relation to the binary classification of the biological aspects (the material reality) of what is referred to here as sexual difference, and suggests the possibility (of the seeming impossibility) of moving beyond the binary frame.

Afterword

1 McNay (1994) argues that Foucault's later work on governmentality and ethics of the self goes some way to surmounting this impasse.

2 See, for example, Jeff Hearn (2004).

Bibliography

Alsop, Rachel, Fitzsimons, Annette, and Lennon, Kathleen (2002) *Theorizing Gender*, Oxford: Polity.

Assiter, Alison (1996) *Enlightened Women: Modernist Feminisms in a Postmodern Age*, London and New York: Routledge.

Barad, Karen (2003) 'Posthumanist Performativity: Toward an Understanding of How Bodies Come to Matter', *Signs: Journal of Women in Culture and Society*, 28 (3): 801–31.

Beauvoir, Simone de (1972) *The Second Sex*, trans. H. M. Parshley, Harmondsworth: Penguin.

Bell, David, Jon Binnie, Julia Cream and Gill Valentine (1994) 'All Hyped Up and No Place to Go', *Gender, Place & Culture* 1: 31–47.

Bell, Vikki (1999a) 'Mimesis as Cultural Survival: Judith Butler and Anti–Semitism', *Theory, Culture & Society*, 16 (2): 133–61.

—— (1999b) 'On Speech, Race and Melancholia: An Interview with Judith Butler', *Theory, Culture & Society*, 16 (2): 163–74.

Benhabib, Seyla (1992) *Situating the Self: Gender, Community and Postmodernism in Contemporary Ethics*, London: Polity.

Benhabib, Seyla, Butler, Judith, Cornell, Drucilla and Fraser, Nancy (1995) *Feminist Contentions: A Philosophical Exchange*, New York and London: Routledge.

Bordo, Susan (1995) *Unbearable Weight: Feminism, Western Culture and the Body*, Berkley, Los Angeles and London: University of California Press.

Bornstein, Kate (1994) *Gender Outlaw: On Men, Women and the Rest of Us*, New York: Routledge.

Braidotti, Rosi (1991) *Patterns of Dissonance: A Study of Women in Contemporary Philosophy*, Cambridge: Polity Press.

Braidotti, Rosi with Butler, Judith (1994) 'Feminism by Any Other Name', *differences: A Journal of Feminist Cultural Studies*, 6 (2 & 3): 27–61.

Bray and Colebrook (1998) 'The Haunted Flesh: Corporeal Feminisms and the Politics of (Dis)Embodiment', *Signs: Journal of Women in Culture and Society*, 24 (11): 35–67.

Brennan, Teresa (1993) *History after Lacan*, London: Routledge.

Breen, Margaret Sönser and Blumenfeld, Warren J. (2005) (eds) *Butler Matters: Judith Butler's Impact on Feminist and Queer Studies*, Burlington and Aldershot: Ashgate.

Butler, Judith (1986) 'Sex and Gender in Simone de Beauvoir's Second Sex', *Yale French Studies*, 72: 34–49. Reprinted in Elizabeth Fallaize (ed.) (1998) *Simone de Beauvoir: A Critical Reader*, London and New York: Routledge.

—— (1987a) *Subjects of Desire: Hegelian Reflections in Twentieth Century France*, New York: Columbia University Press (second edition 2000).

—— (1987b) 'Variations on Sex and Gender: Beauvoir, Wittig and Foucault', in Seyla Benhabib and Drucilla Cornell (eds) *Feminism as Critique: Essays on the Politics of Gender in Late-Capitalist Societies*, Cambridge: Polity.

—— (1988) 'Performative Acts and Gender Constitution: An Essay in Phenomenology and Feminist Theory', *Theatre Journal*, 40 (4): 519–31. Reprinted in Sue–Ellen Case (ed.) (1991) *Performing Feminisms*, Baltimore: Johns Hopkins University Press.

—— (1989a) 'Foucault and the Paradox of Bodily Inscription', *Journal of Philosophy*, 86, Part 11: 601–7.

—— (1989b) 'Gendering the Body: Beauvoir's Philosophical Perspective', in Ann Garry and Marjorie Pearsall (eds) *Women Knowledge and Reality: Readings in Feminist Philosophy*, Boston: Unwin Hyman.

—— (1989c) 'The Body Politics of Julia Kristeva', *Hypatia*, 3 (3): 104–18.

—— (1990a) *Gender Trouble: Feminism and the Subversion of Identity*, New York and London: Routledge.

—— (1990b) 'The Force of Fantasy: Feminism, Mapplethorpe, and Discursive Excess', *differences: A Journal of Feminist Cultural Studies*, 2 (2): 105–25.

—— (1990c) 'Gender Trouble, Feminist Theory, and Psychoanalytic Discourse', in Linda Nicholson (ed.) *Feminism/Postmodernism*, New York and London: Routledge.

—— (1991) 'Imitation and Gender Insubordination', in Diana Fuss (ed.) *Inside/Out: Lesbian Theories, Gay Theories*, New York and London: Routledge.

—— (1992a) 'Contingent Foundations: Feminism and the Question of

Postmodernism', in Judith Butler and Joan W. Scott (eds) *Feminists Theorise the Political*, London and New York: Routledge.

—— (1992b) 'Sexual Inversions' in Domna Stanton (ed.) *Discourses of Sexuality from Aristotle to AIDS*, Ann Arbor: University of Michigan Press.

—— (1992c) 'The Lesbian Phallus and the Morphological Imaginary' in *differences: A Journal of Feminist Cultural Studies*, 4 (1): 133–71.

—— (1992d) 'The Body Politics of Julia Kristeva' in Nancy Fraser and Sandra Lee Bartky (eds) *Revaluing French Feminism: Critical Essays on Difference, Agency and Culture*, Bloomington, IN: Indiana University Press.

—— (1993a) *Bodies that Matter: On the Discursive Limits of 'Sex'*, New York and London: Routledge.

—— (1993b) 'Endangered/Endangering: Schematic Racism and White Paranoia' in Robert Gooding–Williams (ed.) *Reading Rodney King/ Reading Urban Uprising*, New York and London: Routledge.

—— (1993c) 'Poststructuralism and Postmarxism', *Diacritics*, 23 (4): 3–11.

—— (1994a) 'Gender as Performance: An Interview with Judith Butler'. Interview by Peter Osborne and Lynne Segal, *Radical Philosophy*, 67 (Summer): 32–9.

—— (1994b) 'Against Proper Objects', *differences: A Journal of Feminist Cultural Studies*, 6 (2 & 3): 1–26.

—— (1995a) 'For a Careful Reading' in Seyla Benhabib, Judith Butler, Drucilla Cornell and Nancy Fraser (eds) *Feminist Contentions: A Philosophical Exchange*, New York and London: Routledge.

—— (1995b) 'Thresholds of Melancholy' in Steven Galt Crowell (ed.) *The Prism of the Self: Philosophical Essays in Honor of Maurice Natanson*, Dordrecht and Boston: Kluwer Academic Publishers.

—— (1995c) 'Conscience Doth Make Subjects of Us All', *Yale French Studies*, 88: 6–26.

—— (1995d) 'Sovereign Performatives' in Anselm Haverkamp (ed.) *Deconstruction is/in America: A New Sense of the Political*, New York: New York University Press. Reprinted in Eve Koskovsky Sedgwick and Andrew Parker (eds) *Performativity and Performance*, New York: Routledge.

—— (1997a) *Excitable Speech*, New York and London: Routledge.

—— (1997b) *The Psychic Life of Power: Theories in Subjection*, Stanford, CA: University of Stanford Press.

—— (1997c) 'Burning Acts, Injurious Speech: Sovereign Performatives in the Contemporary Scene of Utterance', *Critical Inquiry*, 23 (2): 350–86.

Butler, Judith (1998a) 'Moral Sadism and Doubting One's Own Love: Kleinian Reflections on Melancholia' in Lyndsey Stonebridge and John Phillips (eds) *Reading Melanie Klein*, London and New York: Routledge.

—— (1998b) 'Merely Cultural', *New Left Review*, 227 (Jan. Feb.): 33–44.

—— (1998c) 'Afterword', *Sexualities*, 1 (3): 355–59.

—— (1999) 'Revisiting Bodies and Pleasures', *Theory, Culture & Society*, 16 (2): 11–20.

—— (2000a) 'Subjection, Resistance, Resignification: Between Freud and Foucault' in Walter Brogan and James Risser (eds) *American Continental Philosophy: A Reader*, Bloomington, IN: Indiana University Press.

—— (2000b) 'Competing Universalities' in Judith Butler, Ernesto Laclau and Slavoj Žižek (eds) *Contingency, Hegemony, Universality: Contemporary Dialogues on the Left*, London and New York: Verso.

—— (2000c) *Antigone's Claim: Kinship between Life and Death*, The Wellek Library Lectures, New York: Columbia University Press.

—— (2004) 'Bracha's Eurydice', *Theory, Culture & Society*, 21 (1): 95–100. (First published as the catalogue essay for *The Eurydice Series: Bracha Lichtenberg Ettinger, Drawing Papers* 24, New York: The Drawing Centre Publications, 2002.)

Butler, Judith and Laclau, Ernesto (1997) 'Uses of Equality', *Diacritics*, 27 (1): 2–12.

Butler, Judith and Scott, Joan W. (eds) (1992) *Feminists Theorize the Political*, London and New York: Routledge.

Butler, Judith, Laclau, Ernesto and Žižek, Slavoj (2000) *Contingency, Hegemony, Universality: Contemporary Dialogues on the Left*, London and New York: Verso.

Clement, Catherine and Kristeva, Julia (2003) *The Feminine and the Sacred* (European Perspectives: A Series in Social Thought and Cultural Criticism) trans. Jane Marie Todd, New York: Columbia University Press.

Cornell, Drucilla (1993) *Transformations: Recollective Imagination and Sexual Difference*, London and New York: Routledge.

—— (ed.) (2000) *Feminism and Pornography*, Oxford: Oxford University Press.

De Lauretis, Teresa (1994) *The Practice of Love: Lesbian Sexuality and Perverse Desire*, Bloomington, IN: Indiana University Press.

Derrida, Jacques (1974) *Of Grammatology*, trans. and preface, Gayatori Chakravorty Spivak, Baltimore and London: Johns Hopkins University Press.

—— (1978) 'Structure, Sign and Play in the Discourse of the Human Sciences' in *Writing and Difference*, trans. Alan Bass, Chicago: University of Chicago Press.

—— (1979) *Spurs: Nietzsche's Styles*, trans. Barbara Harlow, Chicago: University of Chicago Press.

—— (1981a) 'The Double Session' in *Dissemination*, trans. Barbara Johnson, Chicago: University of Chicago Press.

—— (1981b) *Dissemination*, trans. Barbara Johnson, Chicago: University of Chicago Press.

—— (1982) *'Différance'*, in *Margins of Philosophy*, trans. Alan Bass, Chicago: University of Chicago Press.

—— (1988) 'Signature, Event, Context' in *Limited Inc.*, edited by Gerald Graff, trans. Samuel Weber and Jeffrey Mehlman, Evanston, IL: Northwestern University Press.

Deutscher, Penelope (1997) *Yielding Gender: Feminism, Deconstruction and Philosophy*, London and New York: Routledge.

Ebert, Teresa L. (1996) *Ludic Feminism and After: Postmodernism, Desire and Labor in Late Capitalism*, Ann Arbor: University of Michigan Press.

Ekins, Richard and King, Dave (eds) (1996) *Blending Genders: Social Aspects of Cross-Dressing and Sex-Changing*, London and New York: Routledge.

Epstein, Julia and Straub, Kristina (eds) (1991) *Body Guards: The Cultural Politics of Gender*, New York and London: Routledge.

Epstein, Steven (1996) 'A Queer Encounter: Sociology and the Study of Sexuality' in Steven Seidman (ed.) *Queer Theory/Sociology*, Oxford: Blackwell.

Esterberg, Kristin G. (1996) ' "A Certain Swagger When I Walk": Performing Lesbian Identity' in Steven Seidman (ed.) *Queer Theory/ Sociology*, Oxford: Blackwell.

Failler, Angela (2005) 'Excitable Speech: Judith Butler, Mae West, and Sexual Innuendo', in Margaret Sönser Breen and Warren J. Blumenfeld (eds) *Butler Matters: Judith Butler's Impact on Feminist and Queer Studies*, Burlington and Aldershot: Ashgate.

Fausto-Sterling, Anne (1993) 'The Five Sexes: Why Male and Female are not Enough', *The Sciences* 3 (2): 20–5.

—— (2000) *Sexing the Body: Gender Politics and the Construction of Sexuality*, New York: Basic Books.

Featherstone, Mike (1992) 'Postmodernism and the Aestheticization of Everyday Life', in Scott Lash and Jonathan Friedman (eds) *Modernity and Identity*, Oxford: Basil Blackwell.

Foucault, Michel (1978) *The History of Sexuality, Volume I, An Introduction*, trans. Robert Hurley, Harmondsworth: Penguin.

176 Bibliography

Foucault, Michel (1984) 'What is Enlightenment?' in Paul Rabinow (ed.) *The Foucault Reader*, Harmondsworth: Penguin.

Freud, Sigmund (1960) *The Ego and the Id*, trans. Joan Riviere, ed. James Strachey. New York: Norton.

Fuss, Diana (1995) *Identification Papers*, London and New York: Routledge.

Garfinkel, Harold (1990) *Studies in Ethnomethodology*, London: Polity.

Gatens, Moira (1996) *Imaginary Bodies: Ethics, Power and Corporeality*, London and New York: Routledge.

Giddens, Anthony (1992) *The Transformation of Intimacy: Sexuality, Love and Eroticism in Modern Societies*, Cambridge: Polity Press.

Goldstein, Richard (1994) 'The Coming Crisis of Gay Rights', *Village Voice*, June: 25–9.

Grosz, Elizabeth (1994) *Volatile Bodies: Towards a Corporeal Feminism*, Bloomington, IN: Indiana University Press.

—— (1995) *Space, Time and Perversion: Essays on the Politics of the Body*, London and New York: Routledge.

Halberstam, Judith (1994) 'F2M: the Making of Female Masculinity', in L. Doan (ed.) *The Lesbian Postmodern*, New York: Columbia University Press.

—— (1998) *Female Masculinity*, Durham, NC: Duke University Press.

—— (2001) 'Oh Behave!: Austin Powers and the Drag Kings', *GLQ: a Journal of Gay and Lesbian Studies*, 7 (3): 425–52.

Hearn, J. (2004) 'From Hegemonic Masculinity to the Hegemony of Men', *Feminist Theory*, 5 (1): 49–72.

Hegel, Georg Wilhelm Friedrich (1977) *Phenomenology of Spirit*, trans. A. V. Miller, Oxford: Oxford University Press.

Heinämaa, Sara (1997) 'What Is a Woman? Butler and Beauvoir on the Foundations of the Sexual Difference', *Hypatia*, 12 (1): 20–39.

Hennessey, Rosemary (1992) *Materialist Feminism and the Politics of Discourse*, London: Routledge.

Heyes, Cressida (2003) 'Feminist Solidarity After Queer Theory: The Case of Transgender', *Signs: Journal of Women in Culture and Society*, 28 (4): 1093–120.

Hood-Williams, John and Harrison, Wendy Cealey (1998) 'Trouble with Gender', *The Sociological Review*, 46 (1): 73–94.

Hughes, Alex and Witz, Ann (1997) 'Feminism and the Matter of Bodies: From de Beauvoir to Butler', *Body and Society*, 3 (1): 47–60.

Hull, Carrie L. (1997) 'The Need in Thinking: Materiality in Theodor W. Adorno and Judith Butler', *Radical Philosophy*, 84: 22–35.

Huffer, Kinda (2001) ' "There is No Gomorrah": Narrative Ethics in Feminist and Queer Theory', *differences: A Journal of Feminist Cultural Studies*, 12 (3): 1–32.

Itzin, Catherine (ed.) (1992) *Pornography: Women, Violence and Civil Liberties*, Oxford: Clarendon Press.

Jackson, Stevi (1995) 'Gender and Heterosexuality: A Materialist Feminist Analysis' in Mary Maynard and June Purvis (eds) *(Hetero)sexual Politics*, London: Taylor & Francis.

Jagger, Gill (2001) 'The Relative Merits of "Writing" and Discourse: Derrida, Foucault, Sexual Difference and the Body' in C. Brina, C. Britton and A. Assiter (eds) *Millennial Visions: Feminisms into the 21st Century*, Cardiff: Cardiff Academic Press.

Kaplan, Ann (1992) 'Review of Gender Trouble', *Signs: Journal of Women in Culture and Society*, 17 (4): 343–8.

Kirby, Vicki (1997) *Telling Flesh: The Substance of the Corporeal*, New York and London: Routledge.

Koestenbaum, Wayne (1991) 'The Queen's Throat: (Homo)sexuality and the Art of Singing' in Diana Fuss (ed.) *Inside/Out: Lesbian Theories, Gay Theories*, New York and London: Routledge.

Kotz, Liz and Butler, Judith (1992) 'The Body You Want: Liz Kotz Interviews Judith Butler' *Artforum*, 31 (3): 82–9.

Kristeva, Julia (1982) *Powers of Horror: An Essay on Abjection*, trans. Leon S. Roudiez, New York: Columbia University Press.

Lecercle, Jean–Jacques (1999) 'Superseding Althusser' (Review of *Excitable Speech*), *Radical Philosophy*, 87 (Jan./Feb.): 41–43.

Lloyd, Moya (1998) 'Politics and Melancholia', *Women's Philosophy Review*, 20: pp. 25–43.

—— (1999) 'Performativity, Parody, Politics', *Theory, Culture and Society*, 16 (2): 195–213.

McIntosh, Mary (1968) 'The Homosexual Role', *Social Problems*, 16 (2): 182–92.

MacKinnon, Catharine (1993) *Only Words*, Cambridge, MA: Harvard University Press.

McNay, Lois (1994) *Foucault*, Cambridge: Polity.

—— (1999) 'Subject, Psyche and Agency: The Work of Judith Butler', *Theory, Culture and Society*, 16 (2): 175–93.

—— (2000) *Gender and Agency: Reconfiguring the Subject in Feminist and Social Theory*, Oxford: Polity.

—— (2003) 'Agency, Anticipation and Indeterminacy', *Feminist Theory*, 42 (2): 139–48.

Mairs, N. (1997) 'Carnal Acts' in Kate Conboy, Nadia Medina and Sarah Stanbury (eds) *Writing on the Body: Female Embodiment and Feminist Theory*, New York: Columbia University Press.

Marcus, Sharon (1992) 'Fighting Bodies, Fighting Words: A Theory and Politics of Rape' in Judith Butler and Joan W. Scott (eds) *Feminists Theorise the Political*, London and New York: Routledge.

Martin, Biddy (1994) 'Sexualities without Genders and Other Queer Utopias', *Diacritics*, 24 (2–3): 104–21.

Matisons, Michelle Renée, (1998) 'The New Feminist Philosophy of the Body: Harraway, Butler and Brennan', *The European Journal of Women's Studies*, 5: 9–34.

Meijer, Irene Costera and Prins, Baukje (1998) 'How Bodies Come to Matter: An Interview with Judith Butler', *Signs: Journal of Women in Culture and Society*, 23 (2): 275–86.

Merck, Mandy, Segal, Naomi and Wright, Elizabeth (eds) (1998) *Coming Out of Feminism?*, Oxford: Blackwell.

More, Kate (1999) 'Never Mind the Bollocks: 2. Judith Butler on Transsexuality. An Interview with Kate More' in Kate More and Stephen Whittle (eds) *Reclaiming Genders. Transsexual Grammars at the Fin de Siècle*, London: Cassell.

More, Kate and Whittle, Steven (eds) (1999) *Reclaiming Genders: Transsexual Grammars at the Fin de Siècle*, London and New York: Cassell.

Morgan, Diane (1999) 'What Does a Transsexual Want? The Encounter between Transsexualism and Psychoanalysis', in Kate More and Stephen Whittle (eds) *Reclaiming Genders. Transsexual Grammars at the Fin de Siècle*, London: Cassell.

Namaste, Ki (1996) ' "Tragic Misreadings": Queer Theory's Erasure of Transgender Subjectivity' in Brett Beemyn and Mickey Eliason (eds) *Queer Studies: a Lesbian, Gay, Bisexual and Transgender Anthology*, New York: New York University Press.

Newton, Esther (1972) *Mother Camp: Female Impersonators in America*, Chicago: University of Chicago Press.

Nietzsche, Friedrich (1969) *On the Genealogy of Morals*, trans. Walter Kaufmann, New York: Vintage.

Parker, Andrew and Sedgewick, Eve Kosofsky (eds) (1995) *Performativity and Performance*, New York and London: Routledge.

Paris is Burning (1990) Director: Jennie Livingstone, Miramax.

Phillips, Adam (1997) 'Keeping It Moving: Commentary on Judith Butler', in Judith Butler, *The Psychic Life of Power: Theories in Subjection*, Stanford, CA: Stanford University Press.

Plummer, Ken (1975) *Sexual Stigma: An Interactionist Perspective*, London: Routledge & Kegan Paul.

Prosser, Jay (1998) *Second Skins: The Body Narratives of Transsexuality*, New York: Columbia University Press.

—— (1999) 'Exceptional Locations: Transsexual Travelogues', in Kate More and Steven Whittle (eds) *Reclaiming Genders: Transsexual Grammars at the Fin de Siècle*, London and New York: Cassell.

Ramazanoglu, Caroline (1995) 'Back to Basics: Heterosexuality, Biology and Why Men Stay on Top', in Mary Maynard and June Purvis (eds) *(Hetero)sexual Politics*, London: Taylor & Francis.

Roen, Katrina (2001) ' "Either/Or" and "Both/Neither": Discursive Tensions in Transgender Politics', *Signs: Journal of Women in Culture and Society*, 27 (2): 501–21.

Rubin, Gayle with Butler, Judith (1994) 'Sexual Traffic', *differences: A Journal of Feminist Cultural Studies*, 6 (2 & 3): 62–99. Reprinted in Mandy Merck, Naomi Segal and Elizabeth Wright (eds) (1998) *Coming Out of Feminism?*, Oxford: Blackwell.

Schaff, Kory (2002) 'Hate Speech and the Problems of Agency: A Critique of Butler', *Social Philosophy Today*, 16: 185–201.

Seidman, Steven (1995) 'Deconstructing Queer Theory or the Under Theorization of the Social and the Ethical' in Linda Nicholson and Steve Seidman (eds) *Social Postmodernism: Beyond Identity Politics*, Cambridge: Cambridge University Press.

—— (1996) *Queer Theory/Sociology*, Oxford: Blackwell.

Shapiro, Judth (1991) 'Transsexualism: Reflections on the Persistence of Gender Ambiguity and the Mutability of Sex' in Julia Epstein and Kristina Straub (eds) *Body Guards: The Cultural Poitics of Gender*, London and New York: Routledge.

Shildrick, Magrit (1997) *Leaky Bodies and Boundaries: Feminism, Postmodernism and (Bio)Ethics*, London and New York: Routledge.

Smith, Robert (1996) 'The Death Drive Does Not Think', *Common Knowledge*, 5(1): 59–75.

Stone, S. (1991) 'The Empire Strikes Back: A Post-Transsexual Manifesto', in J. Epstein and K. Straub (eds) *Body Guards: The Cultural Politics of Gender Ambiguity*, London and New York: Routledge.

Stryker, Susan (1994) 'My Words to Victor Frankenstein above the Village of Chamounix: Performing Transgender Rage', *GLQ: A Journal of Gay and Lesbian Studies*, 1 (3): 237–54.

Stryker, Susan and Whittle, Steven (2006) *A Transgender Studies Reader*, New York and London: Routledge.

Sullivan, Nikki (2003) *A Critical Introduction to Queer Theory*, Edinburgh: Edinburgh University Press.

Tanesini, Alessandra (1998) 'Troubling Philosophy: Interview with Judith Butler', *Women's Philosophy Review*, 18: 7–21.

Tyler, Carole-Ann (1991) 'Boys Will Be Girls: The Politics of Gay Drag' in Diana Fuss (ed.) *Inside/Out: Lesbian Theories, Gay Theories*, New York and London: Routledge.

Walker, Lisa (1995) 'More than Just Skin Deep: Fem(me)ininity and the Subversion of Identity', *Gender, Place and Culture: A Journal of Feminist Geography*, 2 (1): 71–6.

Webster, F. (2000) 'The Politics of Sex and Gender: Benhabib and Butler Debate Subjectivity', *Hypatia*, 15 (1): 1–22.

Weeks, Jeffrey (1997) *Coming Out: Homosexual Politics in Britain from the Nineteenth Century to the Present*, London: Quartet Books.

Weston, Kath (1993) 'Do Clothes Make the Woman? Gender Performance Theory and Lesbian Eroticism', *Genders* 17: 1–21.

Whittle, Steven (1996) 'Gender Fucking or Fucking Gender? Current Cultural Contributions to Theories of Gender Blending' in R. Ekins and D. King (eds) *Blending Genders*, London and New York: Routledge.

—— (2000) *The Transgender Debate: The Crisis Surrounding Gender Identities*, Reading: South Street Press.

—— (2002) *Respect and Equality: Transsexual and Transgender Rights*, London: Cavendish Publishing.

Wilchins, Riki Anne (1997) *Read My Lips: Sexual Subversion and the End of Gender*, Ithaca, NY: Firebrand Books.

Woods, Chris (1995) *State of the Queer Nation*, London: Cassell.

Ziarek, Ewa Plonowska (1997) 'From Euthanasia to the Other of Reason: Performativity and the Deconstruction of Sexual Difference' in Ellen K. Feder, Mary C. Rawlinson and Emily Zakin (eds) *Derrida and Feminism: Recasting the Question of Women*, New York and London: Routledge.

Žižek, Slavoj (2000) 'Class Struggle or Postmodernism? Yes, Please' in Judith Butler, Ernesto Laclau and Slavoj Žižek, *Contingency, Hegemony, Universality: Contemporary Dialogues on the Left*, London and New York: Verso.

Index

agency 9, 12–13, 56, 89–90,
    92–3, 99, 102–5, 116, 162;
    discursive or linguistic 8, 13,
    117, 118, 121, 123–5, 131,
    132; and signification/
    resignification 20, 38–41;
    subject as source of 18, 35–7,
    48, 109, 162
Alsop, Rachel 81, 82, 156
Althusser, Louis 5, 12, 13, 14, 91,
    94, 117, 118, 119, 131, 141,
    160
Assiter, Alison 33
assujetissement 7
Austin, John L. 14, 54, 64, 65,
    66, 117, 124, 131

Beauvoir, Simone de 3, 27, 51,
    52, 53
Being 61
Benhabib, Seyla 37, 86
binary oppositions, critique of
    41–4
biological determinism 2
biology 4, 23, 25, 51, 52, 58, 82
bisexuality 3, 28, 166 n.9
Bodies that Matter 1, 3, 4–5, 6,
    10, 21, 26, 33, 34–5, 36, 37,
    40, 41, 44–6, 53–76 *passim* 79,
    81, 86, 91, 116, 141, 142, 144,
    149
body image 16, 138, 154
the body 1, 17; corporeality of

78–82, 143, 146, 154–5;
    cultural construction of 10, 17,
    18, 31; disabled 81; as
    discursive effect 41, 51, 53, 68;
    economic value of 84; and
    gender acts 26, 27–8; as
    imaginary formation 69, 70,
    71–3, 74, 76–7; intelligibility of
    141–2, 143, 145, 146, 157;
    literality of 146, 147, 148–9;
    materiality of *see* materiality
    of the body; maternal 51, 75; as
    politically constructed 51; as
    product of power/knowledge
    regimes 51, 141, 144; psyche
    and 70–1; and subjectivity 140,
    154–5
Bornstein, Kate 145
Bourdieu, Pierre 112
Braidotti, Rosi 6, 75, 100
Brandon, Teena 133, 153, 170
    n.7
Bray, Abigail 43
butch/femme relationships 32

capitalism 83
categorical imperative 71
censorship 15, 104, 117–18,
    127–8, 133, 134
citation/citationality 10, 40, 41,
    54, 56, 57, 64, 66, 67, 68, 79,
    85
Clement, Catherine 6

Colebrook, Claire 43
conscience 92
constitutive acts 22, 23, 26, 48
construction, social 10, 17, 19, 25, 53–4, 57, 58–9, 142–3
construction/materiality dichotomy 10, 53–4, 57, 58
constructionism/essentialism dichotomy 2, 4, 53–4, 58
Contingency, Universality, Hegemony 13, 106–10
'Contingent Foundations' 60
Cornell, Drucilla 37, 86
corporeality 78–82, 143, 146, 154–5
counter-speech 119, 133, 134, 135
critical masculinity studies 161
critical race theory 15, 117
critique 8, 18, 37–8
cultural determinism 37
culture, subjects as embedded in 36–7

deconstructive approaches 87
Delgado, Richard 122
Derrida, Jacques 1, 44, 61, 69, 117, 124, 160; citation, notion of 41, 54, 57, 64, 66–7, 68; *différence*, notion of 31, 64, 66, 68; dissemination, notion of 43, 44; iteration, notion of 10, 11, 40, 41, 54, 57, 64, 66–7, 68; logocentrism, critique of 64, 165 n.6; performativity, notion of 44, 69; presence, critique of 30, 31, 64, 77, 160; and speech act theory 4, 10, 11, 44, 54, 57, 65–8; temporality, notion of 41, 43, 68
desire 3, 4, 10, 17, 28, 76, 92–3, 101; homosexual 28, 75, 76, 91, 95, 96; and identitification, separation of 76, 98–9; regulation of 91; and subjection 5, 92

Deutscher, Penelope 32, 34
différance 31, 64, 66, 68
disabled bodies 81
discourse: bodily categories as effects of 3, 41, 51, 53, 68; *see also* language; speech; speech act theory; speech acts
dissemination, Derridean notion of 43, 44
domination/resistance binary 42
drag 9, 19, 20, 21, 31, 32, 34–5, 56, 97–9

Ebert, Teresa L. 39, 82–3, 84
economic relations 83–4
ego, bodily 70, 73, 94, 95, 150, 151, 152
Epstein, Steven 25
erotogenicity 70
essentialism 25
essentialism/constructionism dichotomy 2, 4, 53–4, 58
ethnomethodology 22, 24, 25
Excitable Speech 7, 13, 14, 36, 82, 93, 103–4, 115–35 *passim*

Featherstone, Mike 7
femininity 1, 2, 81, 95, 96–7, 161
Feminist Contentions 6, 36, 37
feminist theory 1, 5, 9, 19
foreclosure 12, 13, 91, 100, 106–8, 110, 113
form/matter distinction 59, 63
Foucault, Michel 1, 3, 12, 27, 41, 44, 51, 57, 60, 68, 72, 132–3, 137; on power and subjectivity 3, 12, 53, 68, 90, 92, 99, 132, 141, 160; repressive hypothesis, critique of 4–5, 91
Fraser, Nancy 37, 83, 86
free speech 126, 127
Freud, Sigmund 4, 5, 12, 55, 69, 92, 99, 144, 150; on the bodily ego 70, 73, 94, 152; melancholia, notion of 94–5, 96, 101; on Oedipal relations 76, 94, 95, 99

Fuss, Diana 102, 103

Garfinkel, Harold 24, 25
Gatens, Moira 16, 140, 154
gay and lesbian movement
  110–11
gay and lesbian studies 1, 25
gay relationships 32
gay sexuality 3, 19, 28, 30; *see
  also* homosexuality
gender 1, 10; as an act 26–8;
  biological basis of 4, 23, 82; as
  conditioned by heterosexuality
  1, 17; as discursive effect 41,
  51, 68; materiality of 82–7; and
  melancholia 94–7; as
  performance in a theatrical
  sense 8, 19, 20, 21;
  performativity of 1, 2, 3, 4, 6,
  7, 8–9, 17–49, 54, 94–7; and
  sexuality, constitutive inter-
  relationship 2–3; as social/
  cultural construction 2, 17, 19,
  58
gender constitution 21–6
gender hierarchies 36, 85–6
gender identifications, as
  'phantasmatic' 5, 11
Gender Recognition Act (2004)
  146, 153
Gender Trouble 1, 2, 3, 4, 8, 9,
  17–21, 26–42 *passim* 51, 53,
  97–8, 111–12, 116, 139, 144,
  146–7, 149, 150
Giddens, Anthony 7
Goffman, Erving 22, 23, 24,
  25
Grosz, Elizabeth 6, 16, 140,
  154–6

Halberstam, Judith 145, 152,
  153
Harrison, Wendy Cealey 24, 46,
  47, 48
hate speech 13–15, 82, 104,
  115–18, 121–35; pornography
  as 14, 15, 82, 115, 117–18,

127–31; racist 13, 14, 15, 82,
  104, 115, 117, 122–3, 125–7,
  130, 134–5; state interventions
  and 125–7, 131, 133–4; *see
  also* censorship
Hegel, G.W.F. 5, 12, 92, 94, 101,
  141
Heidegger, Martin 61
heterosexual imperative/
  hegemony 3, 12, 26, 46–7, 48,
  55, 56, 76, 77, 78, 112, 144,
  145, 148, 152, 161
heterosexual morphology 72–3,
  74
heterosexuality 6, 10, 11, 28–32,
  69, 82–3, 86, 87, 147–8, 155;
  compulsory 1, 2, 4, 6, 17, 18,
  19, 20, 21, 28, 32, 34, 44, 51,
  58, 96, 141, 152; and
  homosexual desire, prohibition
  of 95, 96; as ideal, regulatory
  fiction 3–4, 19, 28, 29, 30, 112;
  as imitation and parody 3, 20,
  31–2; as regime of power/
  knowledge 17, 20, 25–6; as
  unstable 3, 32, 42
historical specificity 105–6,
  108
history, subjects as embedded in
  36–7
homophobia 15, 78, 82, 104,
  127, 133
homosexual identification,
  repudiation and incorporation
  of 95, 96
homosexuality 25, 76; feminized
  male 75, 76; masculinized
  female 75, 76; in the military
  13, 111, 115, 132; *see also* gay
  sexuality; lesbian sexuality
Hood-Williams, John 24, 46, 47,
  48
Hughes, Alex 78–9
Hull, Carrie L. 63
humanist view of the subject 18,
  30, 41, 48, 162
Husserl, Edmund 22

ideality/materiality dichotomy 63, 68
identification 10, 12, 55, 57, 69–70, 71, 74, 76, 77, 84, 108, 109; and desire, separation of 76, 98–9; political aspects of 100, 101, 102–3, 137
identity 5, 7; politics of 9, 15, 137; psychic aspects of, and social regulation 5, 12, 82, 89–90, 92, 93, 95–6, 99–100, 104; racial 117; subversion of 18–19, 20, 21, 32–5, 40, 56; trans 16, 138, 139, 143, 145, 157, 162
identity categories 1, 3, 7, 9; cultural construction of 17, 18; denaturalization of 4, 8, 18, 24, 32–3; destabilization of 32, 145; intractability of 12, 13, 19–20, 101, 140; as linguistically constituted 7, 18; 'passionate' attachments to 5, 82, 89; performativity of 7, 9, 17
imaginary 154; alternative anti-heterosexist 75, 76, 77, 145; morphological 71–3, 74, 76–7, 144; symbolic and the 100
imitation 3, 20, 31–2, 98
incest taboo 95, 107
inclusion/exclusion dichotomy 42, 44–5, 46, 106
intelligibility, cultural 141–2, 143, 145, 146, 157
interpellation 5, 12, 13, 91, 93–4, 99, 117, 118–19, 120–21, 122, 141, 160
Irigaray, Luce 1, 6, 11, 57, 59, 75, 76, 144
iteration/iterability 10, 11, 40, 41, 43, 54, 56, 57, 64, 66–7, 68, 113

Jackson, Stevi 39, 82

Kant, Immanuel 71

Kirby, Vicki 63
Kristeva, Julia 6, 11, 51, 75, 144

labelling theory 25
labour, sexual division of 83
Lacan, Jacques 1, 4, 5, 12, 45, 46, 55, 69, 70, 73, 99, 106, 112, 144; on the imaginary 71, 72, 100; on mirror stage 71, 72, 76; on the symbolic 11, 29, 45, 71–2, 74, 100
Laclau, Ernesto 106
language 6, 11, 18, 24, 43, 71, 100; and change 7, 8; and materiality 62–4, 115; and signification 125; and the social 125; and subjectivity 3, 8, 18, 41, 53, 115, 117; vulnerability to 117, 118–23; *see also* discourse; speech; speech act theory; speech acts
lesbian and gay studies 1, 25
lesbian relationships 32
lesbian sexuality 3, 19, 28, 30, 75; *see also* homosexuality
'The Lesbian Phallus and the Morphological Imaginary' 55, 69–70, 72–4
literality of the body 146, 147, 148–9
Lloyd, Moya 89, 101, 102–3
logocentrism 64, 165 n.6

McIntosh, Mary 25
MacKinnon, Catherine 15, 128–9, 130
McNay, Lois 7, 42, 46, 84, 85, 86–7, 90, 100, 101, 104–5, 110, 113
Mairs, N. 81
male-to-female (mtf) transsexuals 140, 143, 155
Mapplethorpe, Robert 128
marriage rights 111
Martin, Biddy 80, 154
masculinity 1, 2, 81, 95, 96–7, 161

materiality 53; genealogy of concept of 10, 59; as linguistic product 62–4; of signification 30, 62–4, 83, 145, 148
materiality of the body 1, 4, 9–10, 11–12, 20, 45, 47, 51–87, 139, 141–6, 159–60; trans bodies 15–16, 20, 78, 80, 138, 146–53, 157; women's bodies 80, 153–4
materiality/construction dichotomy 10, 53–4, 57, 58
materiality/ideality dichotomy 63, 68
maternal body 51, 75
Matisons, Michelle 101
Matsuda, Mari J. 122, 124
matter/form distinction 59, 63
Mead, George Herbert 22
Meijer, Irene Costera 77, 81, 156, 161
melancholia 55, 92, 94–7
melancholic incorporation 12, 94, 95, 98, 99, 100–1, 102
Merleau-Ponty, Maurice 22, 52
metaphysics 143–4; of presence 18, 30–1, 61, 64, 77, 160; of substance 18, 27, 30–1, 61, 160
military 82; homosexuals in 13, 111, 115, 132
mind/body dualism 52
mirror stage 71, 72, 76, 99
More, Kate 141, 145
Morgan, Diane 143
morphogenesis 10, 12, 57, 71, 73, 74, 84
morphological imaginary 71–3, 74, 76–7, 144
morphology 29, 51–2

Namaste, Ki 139
Newton, Esther 31
Nietzsche, Friedrich 1, 3, 9, 11, 12, 18, 22, 30, 51, 92, 94, 160

Oedipal relations 76, 94, 95, 99, 102, 107, 112

oppression of women 48
Orlan 143

pain 70, 82
Paris is Burning (film) 34–5, 85, 153, 170 n.7
parody 3, 9, 19, 31–2, 56; as political strategy 20, 33, 34
patriarchy 29, 47, 48, 83
performance, theatrical models of 4, 8, 19, 21
'Performative Acts and Gender Constitution' 22, 26
performativity 7, 9, 12, 51, 54–5, 74; Derridean notion of 44, 69; of gender 1, 2, 3, 4, 6, 8–9, 17–49, 54, 94–7; of sex 9, 44; of speech and speech acts 4, 13–15, 65–9, 103–4, 115–35; and trans theories and politics 15–16, 137–57
phallogocentrism 1, 11, 17, 18, 19, 20, 34, 51, 58, 141, 152, 161
phallus 11, 72–3; as foundation of symbolic order 72, 74, 77; lesbian 72, 73
'Phantasmatic Identification and the Assumption of Sex' 55, 69–70, 76
phenomenology 8, 22–3, 24, 48, 52, 154
Plato 59
Plummer, Ken 25
political practice 8, 13, 102–5, 110–12, 162
pornography 13, 14, 15, 82, 115, 117–18, 127–31
poststructuralism 1, 9, 18, 21, 29, 30, 53, 62
power 3, 5, 10, 12, 40, 44, 82, 83, 89, 91–2, 112; state 133–4
power/discourse, regimes of 3, 15, 17
power/knowledge, regimes of 17, 20, 25–6, 141, 144, 155
Powers of Horror 51

presence, metaphysics of 18,
30–1, 61, 64, 77, 160
Prins, Baukje 77, 81, 156, 161
Prosser, Jay 16, 138, 139, 140,
145, 146–53
psyche 58, 70–1, 160; and the
social 5, 12, 82, 89–90, 92, 93,
95–6, 99–100, 104, 167 n.4
psychic incorporation of norms
5, 12, 92, 100
The Psychic Life of Power 5, 7,
12, 13, 33, 40, 46, 82, 89, 90,
91–7 *passim*, 99, 101–6 *passim*
113, 116, 141
psychoanalysis 1, 4–5, 10–11, 46,
90–1, 94–7, 101–2, 112, 140,
144, 150, 152, 154, 160; and
materialization of bodies 54–5,
57, 69–74, 76

queer politics 84
queer theory 1, 2, 5, 9, 19, 25,
138, 139, 145, 146, 160, 161
queerness 56, 146, 147, 148

race 56, 164–5 n.3
racial identity and categorization
117
racialization 15, 47, 56, 117
racism 104, 127, 131, 132,
134–5
racist hate speech 13, 14, 15, 82,
104, 115, 117, 122–3, 125–7,
130, 134–5
Radical Philosophy 2, 35
Ramazanoglu, Caroline 82
rape 60–1
recognition 93–4, 141–2, 146;
Hegelian concept of 12, 92, 93,
141
reference/representation
dichotomy 68
referent, and signifier/signified 62
reflexive identity transformation
7
reiteration 36, 40, 42, 43, 113
representation 7, 68

representation/matter dichotomy
42, 43–4
the repressed, return of 46
repression 4–5, 91
resignification 19, 32–3, 35, 72,
99, 101, 103, 104, 105, 113,
132; agency and 20, 38–40
resistance 7, 9, 12, 13, 15, 18, 20,
41, 89–90, 99, 101, 104, 137,
162; and instability of
heterosexuality 3; and
linguistic vulnerability 116–17;
through subversion 19, 35
resistance/domination binary 42
rights 111
Roen, Katrina 138

Sartre, Jean-Paul 27
Schaff, Kory 132, 133
self 41
sex 1, 8, 10, 15, 16, 23, 46, 47,
55, 56; biological basis of 4, 23,
82; as conditioned by
heterosexuality 1, 17; as
cultural regulatory norm 10,
54, 55, 57, 72; as discursive
effect 41, 51, 53, 68;
materiality of 82–7;
performativity of 9, 44; as
political category 29, 52; as
social/cultural construction 2,
17, 25, 31
sex reassignment surgery 138,
139, 152–3
sex/gender distinction 2, 53, 58,
156
sexism 104, 127
sexual difference 6–7, 29, 73,
74–5, 106, 112, 137, 154–6;
and body image 154; duality of
15, 16, 18, 69, 75, 76, 77, 137,
138, 139, 141, 142, 144, 148,
155, 156, 157, 162; gender
hierarchies as product of 86; as
immutable 45, 55, 61;
irreducibility of 155, 157;
ontological status of 39, 61;

psychoanalytic accounts 10, 69, 71; remapping of 141, 157
sexual division of labour 83
sexual innuendo 168 n.1
sexuality 1, 3–4, 28; as discursive effect 3, 51, 53; and gender, constitutive inter-relationship 2–3; psychoanalytic accounts 4–5, 74; repressive hypothesis 4–5; as social/cultural construction 17, 25
signification 11, 18, 20, 54, 69, 71, 72, 74, 77, 78–80, 81, 112, 113; agency and 38–40; and change 7, 8; failure of 44, 46; language and 125; materiality of 30, 62–4, 83, 145, 148; and representation/matter dichotomy 43–4; subjectivity as product of 8
signifier/signified 62
social change 3, 7–8, 9, 12, 13, 15, 18, 19, 20, 35, 56, 137; hate speech analysis and possibility of 131–2, 134–5
social construction 10, 17, 19, 25, 53–4, 57, 58–9, 142–3
social regulation 10, 20, 48, 113, 132; and formation of the psyche 5, 12, 82, 89–90, 92, 93, 95–6, 99–100, 104, 167 n.4
speech: and action, gap between 119, 120; counter- 119, 133, 134, 135; free 126, 127
speech act theory 9, 13, 14, 19, 21, 36, 117, 160; Derrida and 4, 10, 11, 44, 54, 57, 65–8
speech acts 118–20; constative 65; enabling aspects of 15, 116; excitability of 14, 130; illocutionary 119–20, 128; performativity of 13–15, 65–9, 82, 103–44, 115–35; perlocutionary 119, 128; social context of 124–5; temporality of 123, 124, 130

speech/writing opposition 65
Stone, S. 145, 153
stylized repetition of acts 27, 53, 54
subjection 5, 12, 82, 89, 90–4, 99, 101, 103, 160
subjectivity 1, 7–8, 9, 12, 160; and agency 18, 35–7, 48, 109, 162; the body and 140, 154–5; dramaturgical models of 8; as historically and culturally constituted 36–7; humanist view of 18, 30, 41, 48, 162; language and 3, 8, 18, 41, 53, 115, 117; Nietzschean 9; power as productive of 12
Subjects of Desire 5, 92
substance, metaphysics of 18, 27, 30–1, 61, 160
subversion 18–19, 20, 21, 32–5, 40, 56
Sullivan, Nikki 145
symbolic interactionism 22, 25
symbolic order 6, 11, 29, 45, 56, 71–2, 75, 107; phallus as foundation of 72, 74, 77
the symbolic 69, 85, 100, 107, 112

temporality 21, 23, 41, 42–3, 57, 68; of speech acts 123, 124, 130
trans bodies, materiality of 15–16, 20, 78, 80, 138, 146–53, 157
transgender/transexuality 15–16, 24, 80, 137–57

unconscious 13, 99, 100, 102, 105

violence 60–1

Webster, F. 87
Weeks, Jeffrey 25
Whittle, Steven 145–6
Wittgenstein, Ludwig 108

Wittig, Monique 29–31, 39, 44,
    51–2, 60
Witz, Ann 78–9
women: nature of, as culturally
    based 52; oppression of 48
women's bodies 9; materiality of
    80, 153–4; specificities of 80,
    81, 154

writing 65–6, 67

Xtravaganza, Venus 133, 153,
    170 n.7

Ziarek, Ewa Plonowska 44,
    45
Žižek, Slavoj 13, 106–7, 112

Erving Goffman

Greg Smith, University of Salford, UK

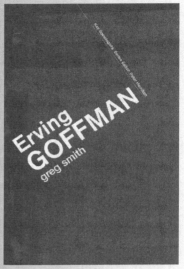

Decades after his death, the figure of Erving Goffman (1922-82) continues to fascinate. Perhaps the best-known sociologist of the second half of the twentieth century, Goffman was an unquestionably significant thinker whose reputation extended well beyond his parent discipline.

A host of concepts irrevocably linked to Goffman's name – such as 'presentation of self', 'total institutions', 'stigma', 'impression management' and 'passing' – are now staples in a wide range of academic discourses and are slipping into common usage. Goffman's writings uncover a previously unnoticed pattern and order in the minutiae of everyday interaction. Readers are often shocked when they recognize themselves in his shrewd analyses of errors, awkwardness and common predicaments.

Greg Smith's book traces the emergence of Goffman as a sociological virtuoso, and offers a compact guide both to his sociology and to the criticisms and debates it has stimulated.

Contents
1. Goffman's Project 2. Origins and Emergence 3. Interaction's Orderliness 4. Framing Experience 5. Asylums 6. Spoiled Identity and Gender Difference 7. Self 8. Methods and Textuality 9. After Goffman

August 2006
HB: 978-0-415-35590-2: **£60.00**
PB: 978-0-415- 35591-9: **£15.99**

Routledge books are available from all good bookshops, or may be ordered by calling Taylor and Francis Direct Sales on +4401264343071 (credit card orders) For more information please contact Gemma-Kate Hartley on 02070175911 or email gemma-kate.hartley@tandf.co.uk

Routledge
Taylor & Francis Group

2 Park Square
Milton Park
Abingdon
Oxfordshire
OX14 4RN
www.routledge.com

Jean Baudrillard

William Pawlett, University of Wolverhampton, UK

This uniquely engaging introduction to Jean Baudrillard's controversial writings covers his entire career, from his early theorisation of the consumer society, his contributions to social semiotics, his neglected masterpiece *Symbolic Exchange and Death*, to his later works on terrorism and 9/11. The book focuses on Baudrillard's central, but little understood, notion of symbolic exchange. Through the clarification of this key term a very different Baudrillard emerges: not the nihilistic post-modernist and enemy of Marxism and feminism that his critics have constructed, but a thinker immersed in the social world and passionately committed to a radical theorisation of it. Baudrillard was a harsh critic of consumerism, of globalisation and of US foreign policy. He mocked the West's desire to unveil, to strip bare, to accumulate and to possess. He attacked pornography, advertising and 'reality' TV, as well as science and information technology, for exemplifying this naïve and ultimately impossible 'dis-illusioning' of the world. Above all Baudrillard sought symbolic spaces, spaces where we might all, if only temporarily, shake off the system of social control. His writing sought to challenge and defy the system. By erasing our 'liberated' identities and suspending the pressures to compete, perform, consume and hate, that the system induces, we might create spaces not of freedom, but of symbolic engagement and exchange.

With lively critical discussion, this groundbreaking text is accessible to an undergraduate audience and will be an invaluable resource for those studying sociology, contemporary social theory, cultural studies and political sociology.

Contents

1. The Object System, the Sign System and the Consumer System 2. The 'Break' with Marxism 3. Symbolic Exchange and Death 4. Simulation and the End of the Social 5. Sexuality, the Body and Seduction 6. Into the Fourth Order 7. Terrorism, 9/11 and War 8. Beyond the Coded Self

November 2007
HB: 978-0-415-38644-9: £65.00
PB: 978-0-415- 38645-6: £16.99

Routledge books are available from all good bookshops, or may be ordered by calling Taylor and Francis Direct Sales on +4401264343071 (credit card orders) For more information please contact Gemma-Kate Hartley on 02070175911 or email gemma-kate.hartley@tandf.co.uk

Routledge
Taylor & Francis Group

2 Park Square
Milton Park
Abingdon
Oxfordshire
OX14 4RN
www.routledge.com

Key Sociologists Series

Edited by Peter Hamilton

The Frankfurt School and its
Critics
The Late Tom Bottomore
2002
PB: 978-0-415-28539-1: £17.99
HB: 978-0-415-28538-4: £65.00

Georg Simmel
David Frisby
2002
PB: 978-0-415-28535-3: £17.99
HB: 978-0-415-28534-6: £65.00

Erving Goffman
August 2006
HB: 978-0-415-35590-2: £60.00
PB: 978-0-415- 35591-9: £15.99

Pierre Bourdieu
Richard Jenkins,
PB: 978-0-415-28527-8: £11.99
HB: 978-0-415-28526-1: £55.00

Emile Durkheim
Professor Kenneth Thompson
PB: 978-0-415-28531-5
HB: 978-0-415-28530-8

Marx and Marxism
2002
Peter Worsley
PB :978-0-415-28537-7: £17.99
HB: 978-0-415-28536-0: £65.00

Auguste Comte
Mike Gane, Loughborough
University, UK
PB: 978-0-415-38542-8 :£15.99
HB: 978-0-415-38543-5: £60.00

Jean Baudrillard
William Pawlett
November 2007
HB: 978-0-415-38644-9: £65.00
PB: 978-0-415- 38645-6: £16.99

Norbert Elias
Robert Van Krieken
1998
PB: 978-0-415-10416-6: £17.99
HB: 978-0-415-10415-9: £75.00

Michel Foucault
Sara Mills
2002
PB: 978-0-415-28532-2: £11..99
HB: 978-0-415-28533-9: £50.00

Max Weber
Dr Frank Parkin
PB:978-0-415-03462-3: £17.99
HB: 978-0-415-28528-5: £80.00

Zygmunt Bauman
Tony Blackshaw,Sheffield Hallam
University, UK
2005
PB: 978-0-415-35504-9: £15..99
HB: 978-0-415-35505-6: £65.00

Jurgen Habermas
M. Pusey
PB: 978-0-415-10451-7: £17.99

Daniel Bell
Malcolm Waters
PB: 978-0-415-10578-1: £24.99
HB: 978-0-415-10577-4: £80.00

Routledge books are available from all good bookshops, or may be
ordered by calling Taylor and Francis Direct Sales on +4401264343071
(credit card orders) For more information please contact Gemma-Kate
Hartley on 02070175911 or email gemma-kate.hartley@tandf.co.uk

Routledge
Taylor & Francis Group

For more information please visit -
http://www.routledgesociology.com/books/
series/Key+Sociologists

2 Park Square
Milton Park
Abingdon
Oxfordshire
OX14 4RN
www.routledge.com

The New Social Theory Reader
2nd Edition

Steven Seidman, State University of New York, USA and Jeffrey C. Alexander, Yale University, USA

This is the first anthology to thematize the dramatic upward and downward shifts that have created the new social theory, and to present this new and exciting body of work in a thoroughly trans-disciplinary manner. It is also the only approach to place the ideas of leading theorists directly into dialogue with one another, while establishing the broad thematic commonalities that tie them together.

In this deeply revised second edition readers are provided with a much greater range of thinkers and perspectives, including new sections on such issues as imperialism, power, civilization clash, health, and performance. The first section sets out the main schools of contemporary thought, from Habermas and Honneth on New Critical Theory, to Jameson and Hall on Cultural Studies, and Foucault and Bourdieu on poststructuralism. The sections that follow trace theory debates as they become more issues-based and engaged:

- The post-foundational debates over morality, justice and epistemological truth
- The social meaning of nationalism, multiculturalism, globalization
- Identity debates around gender, sexuality, race, the self, and post-coloniality

This new edition provides more ample biographical and intellectual introductions to each thinker, and substantial introductions to each of the major sections. It has been finely tuned to ensure readers have the best access to the most recent developments in social theory. The editors introduce the volume with a newly revised interpretive overview of social theory today which, in the previous edition, was recognised as a major intervention in the contemporary intellectual field. *The New Social Theory Reader* is an essential, reliable guide to current theoretical debates.

Contents

Part 1: General theory without foundations NEW CRITICAL THEORY 1. Jurgen Habermas: Contributions to a discourse theory of law and democracy 2. Axel Honneth: Personal identity and disrespect semiotic structuralism 3. Marshall Sahlins: Historical metaphors and mythical realities 4. James Clifford: On ethnographic allegory POSTSTRUCTURALISM 5. Michael Foucault: Power/Knowledge 6. Pierre Bourdieu: Outline of a theory of practice CULTURAL STUDIES 7. Stuart Hall: Cultural studies 8. Frederic Jameson: The political unconscious Part 2: The normative turn JUSTICE 9. Michael Walzer: A defense of pluralism and equality 10. John Rawls: Political liberalism ETHICS 11. Alasdair MacIntyre: Whose justice? Which rationality? 12. Zygmaunt Bauman: Postmodern ethics TRUTH 13. Richard Rorty: Pragmatism, relativism, and irrationalism 14. Seyla Benhabib: Feminism and the question of postmodernism Part 3: Rethinking power PERFORMATIVITY 15. Judith Butler: Imitation and gender insubordination 16. Jeffrey Alexander: Performance and Power DOMINATION/LIBERATION 17. Nancy Fraser: From redistribution to recognition? 18. David Halperin: Queer politics BIOPOLITICS 19. Susan Bordo: The body and the reproduction of femininity 20. Nicolas Rose: The Politics of life itself Part 4: Societies and World Order POSTMODERNITY 21. Jean Baudrillard: Simulcra and simulations 22. David Harvey: The condition of postmodernity CIVIL SOCIETY 23. Jean L. Cohen and Andrew Arato: The utopia of civil society 24. Mary Kaldor: Global civil society MULTICULTURALISM 25. Iris Marion Young: Justice and the politics of difference 26. Will Kymlicka: Multicultural citizenship NATIONALISM 27. Benedict Anderson: Imagined communities 28. Partha Chatterjee: Whose imagined community? WORLD POLITICS 29. Francis Fukuyama: The end of history 30. Samuel Huntington: The clash of civilizations GLOBALISATION 31. Manuel Castells: A new society 32. Ulrich Beck: The cosmopolitan perspective EMPIRE 33. Mahmood Mamdani: From direct to indirect rule 34. George Steinmetz: The new U.S. empire Part 5: Identities SELF 35. Anthony Giddens: Self and society in the late modern age 36. Charles Taylor: The making of modern identity GENDER 37. R.W. Connell: Gender as a structure of social practice 38. Uma Narayan: Westernization and third world feminism SEXUALITY 39. Diana Fuss: Heter Hetero/Homosexuality 40. Steven Seidman: Shifts in normative heterosexuality RACE 41. Michael Omi and Howard Winant: Racial formation 42. Ruth Frankenberg: The mirage of an unmarked whiteness POSTCOLONIALITY 43. Edward Said: Orientalism 44. Paul Gilroy: Postcolonial melancholia.

February 2008
HB: 978-0-415-43769-1: £90.00
PB: 978-0-415- 43770-7: £25.99

Routledge books are available from all good bookshops, or may be ordered by calling Taylor and Francis Direct Sales on +4401264343071 (credit card orders) For more information please contact Gemma-Kate Hartley on 02070175911 or email gemma-kate.hartley@tandf.co.uk

2 Park Square
Milton Park
Abingdon
Oxfordshire
OX14 4RN
www.routledge.com

Routledge
Taylor & Francis Group